CHARLES F. STANLEY

EMOTIONS

CONFRONT THE LIES. CONQUER WITH TRUTH.

HOWARD BOOKS

A Division of Simon & Schuster, Inc.

New York Nashville London Toronto Sydney New Delhi

 Howard Books
A Division of Simon & Schuster, Inc.
1230 Avenue of the Americas
New York, NY 10020

First Howard Books hardcover edition October 2013

HOWARD and colophon are trademarks of Simon & Schuster, Inc.

For information about special discounts for bulk purchases, please contact Simon
& Schuster Special Sales at 1-866-506-1949 or business@simonandschuster.com.

The Simon & Schuster Speakers Bureau can bring authors to your live event. For
more information or to book an event, contact the Simon & Schuster Speakers
Bureau at 1-866-248-3049 or visit our website at www.simonspeakers.com.

All scripture quotations, unless otherwise noted, taken from the New American
Standard Bible. Copyright © 1960, 1962, 1963, 1968, 1971, 1972, 1973, 1975, 1977,
1995 by The Lockman Foundation, La Habra, California. All rights reserved,
http://www.lockman.org.

Scripture quotations marked (TLB) or *The Living Bible* are taken from The Living
Bible (Kenneth N. Taylor; Wheaton, Ill.: Tyndale House, 1997, © 1971 by Tyndale
House Publishers, Inc. Used by permission. All rights reserved.)

Scripture quotations marked (NLT) are taken from the Holy Bible, New Living
Translation, copyright © 1996, 2004, 2007 by Tyndale House Foundation. Used
by permission of Tyndale House Publishers, Inc., Carol Stream, Illinois 60188. All
rights reserved.

Scripture quotations marked (NKJV) are taken from the New King James
Version. Copyright © 1982 by Thomas Nelson, Inc. Used by permission. All rights
reserved.

Interior design by Davina Mock-Maniscalco
Jacket design by Hampton Creative
Jacket art by Corey Lack Pictures

Manufactured in the United States of America

10   9   8   7   6   5   4   3

Library of Congress Cataloging-in-Publication Data

Stanley, Charles F.
    Emotions : confront the lies, conquer with truth / Charles F. Stanley.—First
Howard Books hardcover edition.
      pages cm
1. Emotions—Religious aspects—Christianity. I. Title.
BV4597.3.S735 2013
248.4—dc23   2013021759

ISBN 978-1-4767-5206-8
ISBN 978-1-4767-5208-2 (ebook)

CONTENTS

Contents

EMOTIONS

1

CHOOSING TO TRIUMPH

How God Makes Victory Possible

"I'M SO CONFUSED. WHY WOULD God allow this to happen? Doesn't He care about me?"

"Sometimes I'm completely paralyzed by the thought that people will find out I'm a fraud. And when I consider the future, I am absolutely filled with dread."

"I feel so . . . trapped. I just don't see a way out of all these problems. Why doesn't God help me?"

"Things are so bad right now I don't have the energy to go on. I just want to disappear."

"I feel so alone. No one really loves or understands me. And really, why should they? I'm not so sure I like myself."

"I know God forgives me, but after what I've done, I just can't forgive myself."

* * *

As a pastor for more than five decades, I've heard devastating statements like these repeatedly—the pain of people overwhelmed by deep emotional wounds. We cannot deny it—*emotions are powerful*. We cannot see, taste, or touch them, but we are constantly affected by their forceful presence and the incredible influence they have over us. They are able to alter how we view our day, other people, and even the major events of our lives.

Through our feelings, we have the ability to enjoy amazing triumphs and experience deep fulfillment. In fact, some of the greatest accomplishments in history were fueled by the love, enthusiasm, and compassion of the people who achieved them.

On the other hand, negative emotions left unchecked can lead us to some of the worst tragedies. Greed, pride, envy, fear, and hatred have destroyed lives and brought down empires.

God created you and me with the capacity to experience the full gamut of emotions so we could enjoy life, share our inner being with others, and reflect His image. They were given to us as a gift so we could interact meaningfully with our heavenly Father and the people we know. However, in this fallen world, our feelings have become a mixed blessing. The same capacity that allows us to experience intense, overflowing joy is also the gateway to sorrow so deep and overwhelming that, like Job, we may wish we had never been born (Job 3:3).

> *God created us with the capacity to experience the full gamut of emotions so we could enjoy life, share our inner being with others, and reflect His image.*

Perhaps you have picked up this book because you have seen this in your own life or in the lives of those you love. You have witnessed a pendulum of emotion—highs so great and lows so extreme that you cannot help but question what is going on.

It could also be that you know people who seem to live in abiding peace and contentment, regardless of what they experience. Truly, "The joy of the LORD is [their] strength" (Neh. 8:10). You wonder if you could ever attain such emotional stability and satisfaction.

It's possible that you aren't quite sure what's going on inside of you, and you're just seeking answers. Throughout the years, people have often come to me saying, "Dr. Stanley, I know something isn't quite right, but I can't put my finger on it." I suspect most people have felt this way from time to time. They cannot pinpoint or define their problem, but they feel one exists nonetheless and long to get to the root of it.

Or maybe there is a pervasive agitation that lingers just below the surface of your emotions at all times and for whatever reason it just doesn't go away. Without much warning, your distress springs up and you respond with such intensity that it shocks you and those with whom you're interacting. You never know when this underlying current of anxiety, bitterness, guilt, insecurity, anger, loneliness—or any other destructive feeling—will rear its ugly head and leave destruction in its path. Even worse, you don't understand how to take control of or get rid of it. No doubt, somewhere within you there is a genuine desire to be free of this tyrannical and unpredictable ache in your soul. After all, no one likes to feel bad all the time.

* * *

Our emotions—especially the most damaging of them—can become a dominating force within us if we do not get a hold of them. Of course, most of us like to think that our feelings do not control us. But if we're managing them with anything other than the guidance of the Holy Spirit and the principles of God's Word, we will find it quite difficult to govern how they affect us when the storms of life arise. Given the right combination of circumstances and stressors, our emotions have the potential to motivate us to act recklessly and can also paralyze us from doing what is necessary.

So from the beginning, we see two important dimensions at work in our inmost being:

First, we have an incredible driving force within us that is not easily tamed.

Second, our feelings have a full range of expression: from peace, love, and joy to anxiety, hostility, and despair. From the passions that make life exciting and worth living to those which leave us desolate—wondering how we can go on.

With these in mind, we may wonder, *Can we heal and harness our emotions—taking control of this powerful influence within us? And can we choose to express the positive, life-enhancing emotions rather than the destructive ones?*

THE EMOTIONAL ROLLER COASTER

I recall a lady at one of the churches I pastored who struggled with uncontrolled emotions. She invariably wore her feelings on her sleeve. She was easily offended, often consumed with anger, and frequently grieved over the ways she had been mistreated. Sadly, she had no idea of how this was ruining her life and affecting those around her. She was unaware that she had a choice in the matter.

I can still remember the day I went to lunch with her husband and he expressed his brokenness over their strained marriage. "It's exhausting," he confided wearily.

"What happened?" I asked.

"Nothing unusual," he said. "It's the norm, actually. But some days, I just find it so draining. I never know which version of my wife I'll find when I go to the breakfast table in the morning or what drama will be waiting for me when I get home from work at night. Some evenings, as I reach out to take the doorknob, I just pray, 'God, please give me the strength to face whatever is on the other side of this door.' I dread the emotional firestorm that awaits me. Sometimes she is happy—even giddy with good news, and that's great. But more often than not, she is sad to the point of tears or so extremely angry that she throws the dishes. I never know what to expect. It's as if she is on a roller coaster that never ends. And unfortunately, I'm along for the ride whether I like it or not. It's exhausting."

I had no doubt it was an extremely difficult way to live. "How do you deal with this?" I asked.

He replied, "I try not to say anything. I avoid reacting or responding to what she does because I don't want to aggravate her in any way. I do everything I can to evade becoming the object of her sadness or anger. It's just survival, really."

What a tragedy. Instead of enjoying the wonderful gift of marriage they had been given, this couple was caught in a destructive cycle of outburst and avoidance. The more she would attempt to provoke a response from her husband through her emotional outbursts, the more he would avoid her. And the more he tried to pacify his wife's pain by not engaging with her, the more explosive her responses to him became.

Though both were certainly responsible for some bad decisions, I was always struck by the intense anger and rejection that characterized her interactions with others, which is why I focus on her behavior here. These destructive emotions created a constant tension within her—she was continually plagued with anxiety and suspicion toward those around her. Worst of all, she refused to forgive those who wronged her. If something triggered those old hurts in her memory, she could recall and rekindle intense emotions she had experienced years before within seconds.

She allowed her emotions to rule her, and because of her inability to overcome them or to choose her responses, she was unable to fully enjoy the blessings the Lord had for her. She did not live with a sense of His victorious power. Rather, she endured the terrible bondage of continuous inner churning and restlessness, which kept her from experiencing God's wonderful plan and purpose for her life. Seeing the agony she lived with day in and day out was absolutely heartbreaking.

Certainly she isn't alone. We all go through times of being on edge and distraught. But what I endeavored to teach her and hope to communicate in this book is that as believers, there is no reason for us to live this way. Yes, we may have endured terrible things in our lives and may have been deeply wounded in the process. But there is hope. We can harness our emotions—taking control of this powerful force within us. And we can choose how we respond—opting to express the edifying emotions rather than the destructive ones. Victory is possible. Genuine healing *can* occur if we're willing to allow the Father to set us free.

> *Victory is possible. Genuine healing* can *occur if we're willing to allow the Father to set us free.*

The good news is that Lord *wants* to heal you and those you love. How do I know this? Because we serve the Great Physician—the One who delights in restoring His people, not just emotionally but also spiritually. Look at the promises He has given us in Scripture:

- "I, the LORD, am your healer." (Ex. 15:26)
- "I have heard your prayer, I have seen your tears; behold, I will heal you." (2 Kings 20:5)
- "The LORD is near to the brokenhearted and saves those who are crushed in spirit. Many are the afflictions of the righteous, but the LORD delivers him out of them all." (Ps. 34:18–19)
- "They cried out to the LORD in their trouble; He saved them out of their distresses. He sent His word and healed them, and delivered them from their destructions." (Ps. 107:19–20)
- "The LORD . . . heals the brokenhearted and binds up their wounds." (Ps. 147:2–3)
- "He was pierced through for our transgressions, He

was crushed for our iniquities; the chastening for our well-being fell upon Him, and by His scourging we are healed." (Isa. 53:5)

- "'I will heal him; I will lead him and restore comfort to him . . . creating the praise of the lips. Peace, peace to him who is far and to him who is near,' says the LORD, 'and I will heal him.'" (Isa. 57:18–19)
- "'I will restore you to health and I will heal you of your wounds,' declares the LORD." (Jer. 30:17)
- "Peace I leave with you; My peace I give to you; not as the world gives do I give to you. Do not let your heart be troubled, nor let it be fearful." (John 14:27)

The Father is uniquely *able* to give us the victory over the damaged emotions we have. And because we cannot become the healthy, fruitful believers He wants us to be until we learn to control our feelings, we know for certain He is *willing* to help us. We are confident of this because we are assured the Lord desires for us to experience the fullness of His wonderful plans for our lives. He says, "I know the plans that I have for you . . . plans for welfare and not for calamity to give you a future and a hope" (Jer. 29:11). Truly, we serve a loving God who will not fail to lead us to freedom if we trust in Him (John 8:32).

THE FIRST STEP

Of course, in order to have a relationship with the Lord at all, the first thing we must be prepared to do is admit we cannot help ourselves. This is true in every area of our interactions with the Father—even the ability to experience Him or receive His healing. Why? Because there is something deep within us that completely cuts us off from His presence.

> *In order to have a relationship with the Lord at all, the first thing we must be prepared to do is admit we cannot help ourselves.*

Habakkuk 1:13 reports, "Your eyes are too pure to approve evil, and You cannot look on wickedness with favor." Because God is absolutely holy, He is separated from all sin—all the things we have done wrong, the mistakes we have made, and the ways we've failed to do His will.

Usually, we recognize our sins right away because they are all too evident to us. We are aware of all the selfish acts and unwise decisions that make us feel unclean and unworthy. We also realize that no matter how much good we do, our mistakes stay with us. We cannot rid ourselves of them. We see firsthand that what the Bible says is true, "All our righteous deeds are like a filthy garment" (Isa. 64:6). We can try to cover ourselves with good works, but they will never be sufficient to cleanse the foulness we feel within our hearts. No matter how hard we try, our sins continue to follow us.

Why is this? It is because "the wages of sin is death" (Rom. 6:23).

When we do wrong, we feel the sentence of death within us. So not only are we separated from God, but we feel the destructive consequences of our sinful actions taking hold at the very core of our being.

Thankfully, our heavenly Father had mercy on us. Knowing that we could never help ourselves, God took the initiative to forgive our sins and restore our relationship with Him (Rom. 5:8). How did He do so? By coming to Earth in the form of a Man—as Jesus—to die on the cross as the sacrificial, substitutionary payment for all our sins. He wipes them away completely. "As far as the east is from the west, so far has He removed our transgressions from us" (Ps. 103:12).

And to show us definitively that He was absolutely victorious over sin and death—that what He did worked—Christ rose triumphantly from the grave after three days. Because of His bodily resurrection, we know for certain that Jesus will faithfully fulfill His promise to give us eternal life.

What Christ did on the cross solved our problem of being separated from God. An eyewitness of the crucifixion and resurrection, the apostle Peter explained to a crowd of faithful Jews who had gathered in Jerusalem:

"Jesus the Nazarene, a man attested to you by God with miracles and wonders and signs which God performed through Him in your midst, just as you yourselves know—this Man, delivered over by the predetermined plan and foreknowledge of God, you nailed to a cross by the hands of godless men and put Him to death. But God raised Him up again, putting an end to the agony of death, since it was impossible for Him to be held in its power. . . .

"God has made Him both Lord and Christ—this Jesus whom you crucified." . . . Now when they heard this, they were pierced to the heart, and said to Peter and the rest of the apostles, "Brethren, what shall we do?" Peter said to them, "Repent, and each of you be baptized in the name of Jesus Christ for the forgiveness of your sins; and you will receive the gift of the Holy Spirit. For the promise is for you and your children and for all who are far off, as many as the Lord our God will call to Himself." And with many other words he solemnly testified and kept on exhorting them, saying, "Be saved" (Acts 2:22–24, 36–40).

Peter proclaimed the truth of Christ's provision to the faithful Jews, who were used to pleasing God by their adherence to the Law of Moses. Day after day, year after year, they made sacrifices in accordance with that Law, hoping it would be sufficient to earn them the Lord's favor. However, it was never enough. Each new day brought new temptations, sins, and violations of God's holy standards. It seemed hopeless that anyone could truly have a relationship with the Father. And it really was impossible because "There is none righteous, no, not one" (Rom. 3:10). It was unattainable, that

Jesus died on the cross and rose from the grave to make us holy and acceptable to Him once and for all.

is, until Jesus died on the cross and rose from the grave to make us holy and acceptable to Him once and for all.

Romans 5 explains, "Since we have been made right in God's sight by faith in His promises, we can have real peace with Him because of what Jesus Christ our Lord has done for us. . . . Now we rejoice in our wonderful new relationship with God—all because of what our Lord Jesus Christ has done in dying for our sins—making us friends of God" (vv. 1, 11, TLB).

When you trust Jesus as your Savior, you accept the fact that He makes you holy—fully capable of experiencing God's loving presence and healing. You rely upon Jesus' perfect provision of salvation, which means you have confidence in Him to forgive your sins, deliver you from the sentence of death, restore your relationship with the Father, and bless you with eternal life.

As I said, Jesus does it all for you because He knows you cannot do it yourself. Ephesians 2:8 makes it clear, "By grace you have been saved through faith; and that not of yourselves, it is the gift of God." Therefore, the only thing you must do is accept His gift of salvation by faith. Romans 10:9 promises, "If you confess with your mouth Jesus as Lord, and believe in your heart that God raised Him from the dead, you will be saved."

Of course, you may be thinking, *Why is he introducing all this about salvation now—right at the beginning of a book about emotions?* There are two reasons.

1. *Trusting Jesus Comes First*

If you cannot trust Jesus enough to save you, then nothing I write here will do you any good. You cannot even begin to have fellowship with God until your sins are forgiven once and for all through faith in Christ.

This is because when Jesus saves you, He sends His Holy Spirit to live within you and teach you. The Holy Spirit is the One who searches your heart and mind—repairing your brokenness, counteracting wrong beliefs, and enabling you to overcome your circumstances. Without a relationship with Him, there can be no true emotional healing. Without the Holy Spirit empowering you, you cannot have victory over your feelings.

> *The Holy Spirit is the One who searches your heart and mind—repairing your brokenness, counteracting wrong beliefs, and enabling you to overcome your circumstances.*

Therefore, if you have never accepted Jesus as your Savior, I urge you to do so now. It is not difficult—He has done all the work for you. All you must do is confess your belief in Him either in your own words or with the following prayer:

Jesus, please forgive my sins and save me from eternal separation from God. By faith, I accept Your work and death on the cross as sufficient payment for my sins. I rejoice that Your resurrection from the dead shows Your complete victory over sin and death—making me holy and acceptable in God's sight. Thank You for providing the way for me to have a relationship with my heavenly Father and eternal life. Thank You for hearing my prayers and sending Your Holy Spirit to heal me in areas where I have been wounded and my emotions have been damaged. Please give me the strength and wisdom to walk in the center of Your will now and forevermore. In Your holy and precious name I pray, Lord Jesus. Amen.

2. Saving Faith Models Trust in God

The second reason I am talking about salvation at the beginning of a book about emotions is because your saving faith is a model for the kind of trust in God you'll need for healing.

Let me explain. Just as you cannot save yourself, you cannot change your feelings. Just as you must fully rely upon Jesus to make you holy and acceptable for a relationship with Him, it is likewise necessary for you to depend on Him to completely restore your emotional health. Your responsibility is simply to obey Him as He directs you. He does the rest.

This is because God knows you perfectly, sees your hidden scars, and fully understands the reason you react to situations as you do. On the other hand, you may believe that you can try hard enough to get better or heal by sheer willpower; however, that will never be enough. Why? Because you do not know which of your habits and response patterns have been formed in order to protect your damaged emotions—and you don't have a way of finding this out apart from the work of the Holy Spirit. And even if you could know what behaviors and reactions to target, you wouldn't have an effective plan for how to supplant them—destroying their deepest roots within you and replacing them with the truth that heals you.

Recall the couple I described earlier. The wife certainly was not trying to drive away her husband through her emotional outbursts. Likewise, the husband was not seeking to hurt his wife by avoiding her. However, neither was responding to the other beneficially. Their relational patterns were making their problems far worse, not better. And the harder they tried, the more their broken, wounded ways alienated each other.

Unfortunately, this is our reality. We simply don't know how to deal with the issues that lie buried so deep within our souls. This is because of what we find in Proverbs 16:25, "There is a way which seems right to a man, but its end is the way of death." Thankfully, our God is more than willing to make "the path of life" (Ps. 16:11) known to us. He knows exactly how to heal us, and as we saw in Scripture, He is more than willing to do so.

> *Our God is more than willing to make "the path of life" (Ps. 16:11) known to us.*

YOU HAVE AN EXAMPLE OF TRIUMPH

Before we go on, however, there is something that must be made abundantly clear: If you are struggling with difficult feelings, *you are not alone.*

If you are struggling with difficult feelings, you are not alone.

One of the most devastating things about our injured emotions is how isolated they make us feel. They can make us think there is something wrong with us—that we are weak, alone, incapable of improving, and that no one will want to be around us. We wonder if we're being punished—set apart from the rest of humanity to suffer. We may even begin to believe that no one in history has ever felt as incredibly low and terrible as we do, and that we're damaged as no one else has ever been. Nothing could be further from the truth.

I live in Atlanta, which is infamous for its exceedingly slow rush hour. Waiting in bumper-to-bumper traffic often gives me time to read the stickers on fellow commuters' automobiles. Many leave me groaning rather than laughing. However, I recently saw one that said, "Nobody gets out of life alive." The author could have easily added, "And nobody gets through this life without some scars." Just as sure as all of us will someday face death, is the certainty that we will all face painful circumstances that will wound us deeply.

It is a universal fact: every person faces hard times, obstacles, disappointments, and some degree of emotional pain throughout his or her life. If you haven't yet faced any difficulties—trust me, you will. Unfortunately, in this fallen world, they cannot be avoided.

The great King David often felt emotional agony, which we can read about in Psalms. Yes, he had some astounding times of joy and success. But he also suffered staggering betrayals, unbearable losses, and heartrending failures. He wrote, "I am bent over and greatly bowed down; I go mourning all day long. . . . I am benumbed and badly crushed; I groan because of the agitation of my heart" (Ps. 38:6, 8). His inspiring hymns have often comforted the hurting because he understood firsthand the pain all of us feel at one point or another.

The apostle Paul suffered greatly as well. He said, "We were burdened excessively, beyond our strength, so that we despaired even of life" (2 Cor. 1:8).

Even our perfect, sinless Savior, Jesus, felt profound and overwhelming anguish. He said, "My soul is deeply grieved, to the point of death" (Matt. 26:38).

No, you are certainly not alone in your feelings. I say all this because there have been others throughout history who have felt as you do and who've found victory over their emotions. Just as it was feasible for them, it is possible for you as well. They are your example. As I said, we can take control of the driving force of emotions within us and we can also choose how we respond. God taught them how to do so, and He will show you, too.

THE PATH TO VICTORY

So how did the saints of old triumph over these devastating emotions? It was through the principle David wrote about in Psalm 26:2–3. He said, "Examine me, O LORD, and try me; test my mind and my heart. For Your lovingkindness is before my eyes, and I have walked in Your truth." In other words, David overcame his destructive emotions by asking God to reveal any wrong way of thinking within him and replacing it with the Lord's facts and unfailing principles.

Paul explained it like this in 2 Corinthians 10:5: "We are destroying speculations and every lofty thing raised up against the knowledge of God, and we are taking every thought captive to the obedience of Christ." These men rejected their destructive patterns of behavior and thinking—preferring instead to believe what God said about them above all else.

Napoleon Hill, author and advisor to President Franklin Delano Roosevelt, summarized this principle when he said, "If you direct your thought and control your emotions, you will ordain your destiny." In other words, if you will deliberately govern what you think, you will transform your emotions—you will manage them instead of them ruling over you. And as you choose how you feel and bring your beliefs in line with what God says about you, the Lord works to make you into the person He created you to be.

So let me ask you: What are the most painful experiences you've had and what wounds remain from them? What emotions assail you as a result of those difficulties? Now consider this carefully:

When those feeling rise up within you, what are the thoughts that play over and over again in your mind? Are there messages you've come to accept as a result of the pain you've experienced?

I ask you this so you can deal with the problems and find victory in them. If the messages that play repeatedly in your mind do not line up with God's Word, they are false and must be supplanted. This means you must confront the treacherous beliefs directly in order to have control over them and be able to choose your response.

Therefore, as we explore difficult feelings such as fear, rejection, bitterness, guilt, and despair, we are also going to discuss how to overcome them individually. These will vary some from chapter to chapter, but the basic components to triumphing over your emotions include the following:

1. Experiencing the New Birth

As I said previously, healing begins with a relationship with God through faith in Jesus' saving work on the cross. That does not mean your emotions are repaired immediately when you accept Him as Savior. Sadly, there are many believers who have never enjoyed that deep restoration. Rather, you receive the Lord's presence with you through His Holy Spirit, which means you have everything you require to be victorious.

Ephesians 1 tells us, "God . . . has blessed us with every spiritual blessing in the heavenly places in Christ" (v. 3). These include a *new nature* (v. 4), *identity* (v. 5), *future* (v. 11), *purpose* (v. 12), *hope* (v. 18), and *power* (v. 19). As we look at the falsehoods that continue to damage our emotions, we will see how these spiritual blessings—which we receive at salvation—counteract them.

Again, if you have never accepted Jesus as your Savior, I pray you will. Do not remain in bondage, friend; a better life is within reach. Invite God into your life and allow Him to heal you.

2. Examining the Thoughts That Dominate Your Life

As we've discovered, emotional brokenness does not heal automatically. Although we're often told, "Time heals all wounds," it simply isn't true. The passing of the days, months, and years may cause the memory of the offense to fade to a degree, but the pain it caused becomes part of us, tainting how we view the world and respond to our circumstances. This is because time itself has no power to heal; it cannot remove the unhealthy thought patterns formed when our wounds are created—it cannot even identify them.

Only the Father can pinpoint where we've been injured and what destructive coping mechanisms we've developed to protect ourselves. Only He recognizes what lies we believe about ourselves and which attitudes keep us in bondage.

This is one of the reasons we study the consequences of feelings such as fear, guilt, and so forth. Because once we realize how these emotions affect us, we can then trace them back to their roots.

I've had all sorts of people come up to me after Sunday morning services and say, "I never knew that was an issue for me. But when I heard you list the effects, I realized it's a real problem in my life. That's what I have been struggling with—I just didn't know it."

When we discover what is actually affecting us, we can then begin to recognize what it was in our past that created our misunderstanding about who we are. This is the work of the Holy Spirit in us—He exposes the false messages that drive our identity, decisions, and interactions with others. God then unearths those false beliefs so He can replace them with truth and make us whole.

This is the work of the Holy Spirit in us— He exposes the false messages that drive our identity, decisions, and interactions with others.

This leads to the third component of healing your emotions.

3. Exchanging Your Thought Patterns

Once the deceptive ideas that fuel our feelings are revealed, they must be replaced by a godly thought process. This is not something that can be developed overnight, of course; it takes time to learn. But the most effective thing we can do is read Scripture, which not only familiarizes us with what the Father thinks but also teaches us His principles, how He expresses emotion, and the method by which He makes decisions.

After all, who better to learn from than the Lord God Himself? "With Him are wisdom and might; to Him belong counsel and understanding" (Job 12:13). When we immerse ourselves in God's Word, He begins to renew us—changing the way we see things and giving us His perspective of situations. He reveals the conditions that trigger our damaged emotions and teaches us to respond in a manner that builds us up, rather than tears us down. And He shows us how to enjoy the abundant life He created us for (John 10:10).

Truly, when the Father shows us how to think and control our emotions, we begin to enjoy life at its very best. No wonder King David wrote, "Bless the LORD, O my soul, and forget none of His benefits; who pardons all your iniquities, who heals all your diseases; who redeems your life from the pit, who crowns you with lovingkindness and compassion; who satisfies your years with good things" (Ps. 103:2–5).

Of course, if we really want to exchange our thought patterns for good, we must actively engage in this next component.

4. Exercising the Powerful Privilege of Prayer

If you've listened to me for any amount of time or read any of my other books, you know how absolutely essential I believe prayer is to our lives. This is because prayer is an intimate conversation with the God of all that exists, and your relationship with Him determines the impact of your life and the influence you have with those around you. Time alone with Him is vital for the growing believer. It is also crucial if we desire true emotional healing.

The Word of God is powerful on its own. But I have found that there is nothing more life-changing than getting on my knees, opening Scripture, and waiting before the Father with an attitude of listening. It is astounding what the Lord reveals when we come before Him in love and reverence, and how He heals the brokenness within us. This is why I often say, "We stand tallest and strongest on our knees." Because when we humble ourselves before the God of the universe, He helps us and lifts us up (1 Pet. 5:5–6).

I have found that there is nothing more life-changing than getting on my knees, opening Scripture, and waiting before the Father with an attitude of listening.

Therefore, in the pages to come, we will examine some of the godly thought patterns that can help you overcome your emotions so you can enjoy the wonderful blessings God has for you. But I will also challenge you to seek the Father's face for true, lasting healing.

5. Expecting God's Healing to Begin Immediately

Finally, throughout this book, I will encourage you to endure courageously, knowing that the Holy Spirit is already at work in your heart, though you may not be aware of what He has accomplished. In fact, you may not feel any better for a while—but that is the point. It is your emotions that are damaged, and some deep spiritual surgery is needed.

As God transforms the way you think, everything within you may want to fight against what you're learning and your pain may even intensify. This is because you are working on areas that are profoundly battered and bruised.

Persevere anyway. It is only temporary. Exercise your ability to endure despite your feelings because you're finally on the path to taking control of your life and experiencing the edifying emotions the Father made you to enjoy. Your effort is not in vain; this struggle is worthwhile. And you have been given a divine guarantee: if you have faith in God and obey Him, He will bless you every single time. He *will* heal your emotions. Freedom is just around the corner.

God will heal your emotions. Freedom is just around the corner.

So what are the painful wounds that you wrestle with daily? What false messages are driving your emotions? What ache do you feel in your heart? Perhaps they spring immediately to mind. Or maybe you just don't know. Either way, spend some time in prayer now, asking God to prepare you for the journey that is ahead.

Father, how grateful I am for all You have done for me. Thank You for saving me, giving me life, and providing me with every spiritual blessing in Christ Jesus. I also give You thanks for helping me find the path to victory over these feelings that are so painful and overwhelming. I confess that I have allowed them to rule me—hurting my relationships, destroying my joy, and preventing me from fully understanding the purposes You have planned for me. Thank You for forgiving me, Father. Please reveal the destructive thought patterns so I can repent of them and walk in the center of Your will.

I bring my damaged emotions to You right now and ask You to deliver me from them.

Father, thank You for hearing my prayers and healing my damaged emotions. It is my heart's desire to respond in a manner that honors You and brings You glory. I am so grateful You are teaching me to take control of my emotions so I can become the joyful, fruitful believer You created me to be. Thank You for healing me, restoring my hope, and giving me purpose, Lord God. I praise You for Your great love and for leading me to freedom. In Jesus' name I pray. Amen.

QUESTIONS FOR
PERSONAL REFLECTION AND GROUP STUDY

1. Which emotions do you experience most powerfully when relating with your friends and family members? Is there any relationship that raises particularly negative emotions? Why do you think that is?

2. Do you ever feel alone when you experience negative emotions? How have you coped with those feelings of loneliness? Is this manner of coping working for you? Why or why not?

3. What do you think is the one thing that is preventing you from fully experiencing God's healing in your life?

4. Do you believe your faith in Christ's salvation is important for the restoration of your emotional health? Why or why not?

5. In the list of Bible promises regarding God's provision of healing, are there particular verses that bring you comfort?

6. Have you ever tried to manage your feelings in any of the ways described in this chapter? What was the result?

7. Through the years, have you received the genuine healing that can come only from the Father? Are you hopeful you can experience it now? Why or why not?

8. Which of the steps in triumphing over your emotions are you ready to apply to your life and thought patterns immediately?

2

WHAT'S GOING ON HERE?

God's Purpose for Our Emotions

WOULDN'T LIFE BE SIGNIFICANTLY EASIER if we didn't have to struggle with our feelings? Wouldn't the problems we face be far more manageable if our emotions weren't involved? Think about it. It usually isn't our circumstances that devastate us; rather, it's the memories and sentiments they stir up that cause us to become disheartened. Our moods can transform any minor trial we face into a truly intense and demoralizing battle.

For example, when dismissed from a job, what is it that really troubles us? Generally, it is that we feel some level of rejection and fear of the future—often wrestling with the wounds caused by other losses we've faced. We wonder if anyone will ever hire us or find us competent again. Of course, we have the assurance "My God will supply all your needs according to His riches in glory in Christ Jesus" (Phil. 4:19). As believers, we have absolutely no reason to suspect that the Father will ultimately fail to supply what we need. But our emotions undermine the sense of security we should have in God's perfect provision.

Likewise, when waiting for the Lord to fulfill a heart's desire or promise to us, why do we distrust Him? Why don't we think about all the times God has kept His word and proven Himself faithful? Isn't it because of our feelings—because we doubt ourselves and our circumstances? Don't we focus on the instances when our hopes were disappointed? Aren't we bombarded with feelings of inadequacy and unworthiness? When waiting on the Father, we could easily claim promises such as the one we find in Romans 8:31–32: "If God is for us, who is against us? He who did not spare His own Son, but delivered Him over for us all, how will He not also with Him freely give us all things?" But our emotions often stand in direct opposition to our faith in the Lord and what He is achieving for us.

Our emotions often stand in direct opposition to our faith in the Lord and what He is achieving for us.

Sadly, our emotions can even keep us from obeying God. Not long ago, I spoke with a man who admitted to me that when he was young, the Lord called him to become a pastor. It had been more than thirty years, but he told me he could still remember how strong and powerful the Father's call was. From his demeanor, it was easy to tell he was wracked with regret that he had failed to pursue it.

"What kept you from obeying Him?" I asked.

He didn't hesitate in replying, "I was scared."

"What of?" I asked.

"I was petrified at the very idea of public speaking. The thought of getting up in front of a crowd still causes my mouth to go dry and my heart to pound. I couldn't imagine preaching."

What a tragedy. This man missed the awesome privilege of serving God because of fear. I could see the lack of fulfillment and disappointment on his face. He would always be left wondering what the Lord could have done through him—what people could have been saved and what lives could have been transformed had he been faithful. Yet this is what our emotions sometimes do—they prevent us from obeying God and trusting the excellent plans He has for our lives.

So why would our loving heavenly Father give us our feelings in the first place? Why would He equip us with the capacity to feel such terrible sorrow, rejection, and despair when these emotions can be so destructive? What was His purpose?

THE GIFT OF EMOTIONS

As I suggested in the previous chapter, the Father formed us with the ability to experience emotions so we could enjoy life, interact meaningfully with others, and mirror His likeness. But from the time sin entered the world, painful feelings surfaced that had not been observed previously in the Garden of Eden.

After they disobeyed God by eating the fruit that was forbidden, Adam and Eve expressed shame at their nakedness (Gen. 3:7) and dread toward the Lord (Gen. 3:10)—sentiments they had not felt beforehand in the biblical record (Gen. 2:25). This doesn't mean they did not have the capacity to experience these emotions until the fall. In fact, we know that even before the fall, the Father saw the possibility that Adam would face loneliness and took action (Gen. 2:18). Rather, it means that one of the consequences of their sin was to awaken these negative feelings in them.

Likewise, the fall does not make our emotions any less of a gift from God. Instead, it signifies that it is even more important for us to understand the reasons the Father gave us our feelings and to live within the healthy boundaries He has given us for them.

> *It is important for us to understand the reasons the Father gave us our feelings and to live within the healthy boundaries He has given us for them.*

For example, before Adam sinned, he was never frightened of spending time with God. He would walk with the Father, learn from Him, and enjoy His presence. But after the fall, Adam was so afraid of being seen by the Lord that he hid himself (Gen. 3:10).

Ever since then, the Father has had to encourage us repeatedly: "Do not fear" (Gen. 15:1), "love the LORD your God" (Deut. 6:5), and "walk in His ways" (Deut. 8:6). Like Adam, the consequences of sin within us make us feel vulnerable and exposed when we meet with God, so we may hide ourselves from Him as a result. But realizing this, we can make a decision to do what we know will heal us—which is to "draw near with confidence to the throne of grace, so that we may receive mercy and find grace" (Heb. 4:16).

With this in mind, let us take a closer look at why the Lord gave us the ability to feel.

1. So We Can Enjoy Life

The first reason we were created with emotions is so we can enjoy and appreciate the lives God has given us. Just imagine what our existence would be like if we couldn't experience love, happiness, excitement, fulfillment, or surprise. Think about how awful it would be to have no internal reaction or affective response when a child is born, a victory is won, or great goals are achieved. To not feel joy, satisfaction, or delight in these events would be a tragedy indeed. We wouldn't be living; we would simply exist with nothing to motivate us but our physical needs.

But perhaps you wonder, *Why didn't God just give us the affirming emotions? Why did He give us the painful ones as well?* This is a good question—similar to one theologians and philosophers have wrestled with for centuries: *Why would our gracious Father allow grief and suffering?*

As we just discussed, we live in a fallen world, and the enemy takes the aspects of our lives that the Lord meant for good—especially our emotions—and distorts them in order to cause us pain and keep us from serving God. However, the Father created us with the ability to experience negative emotions for some very practical and advantageous reasons that we cannot ignore. In fact, they are crucial for our daily lives.

For example, we can probably agree that a healthy fear of lions, grizzly bears, and active volcanoes is good. It protects us from approaching them foolishly without the proper precautions and losing our lives.

Likewise, the sorrow we feel when a loved one passes away not only helps us understand how valuable life is but also teaches us to appreciate the time we have with people.

However, I think the most important reason we have been given the more difficult emotions is because without them, we might not realize we need God. Most people don't seek the Lord when they are happy—at least, not in the beginning of their relationship with Him. They do not automatically ascribe the blessings they receive to His kind and generous hand.

Without our emotions, we might not realize we need God.

Rather, it is in the difficult times that the majority of people look to the Father for help. Perhaps they have hit rock bottom, the painful consequences of their sins overwhelm them, and they recognize they need His divine deliverance. Or maybe someone they love is suffering and there is nothing they can do other than pray. It could even be that a persistent emptiness or uneasiness continually assails their soul, so they search for answers. Whatever the case, the emotional distress gets their attentions and drives them to the Lord, who then offers them a gift they may not have realized they needed—eternal life.

I realize this is a very brief treatment of the topic of suffering, and that to do it justice, we must look into it more deeply. I promise we will do so in the pages to come. We will also examine how the enemy warps our emotions in order to overwhelm us and keep us in bondage.

The point is, the Father can teach us to enjoy and appreciate our lives even through our negative emotions. Therefore when we experience them, we must remember that He never intended for us to remain in them. Rather, their purpose is to protect us, show us what is good, and make us aware of what is really important and fulfilling.

2. So We Can Meaningfully Relate to Others

Many things divide people: cultures, tastes, politics, beliefs, and what have you. But what binds us together—what helps us understand each other and connects us to one another—is our emotions. I've often been amazed that the sermons that are meaningful to people in the United States are just as poignant to those in Venezuela, Kenya, Lebanon, Bulgaria, and Malaysia, even though our societies are so diverse. Of course, it is the power of the Holy Spirit that makes those messages powerful and all glory goes to God. But He uses the commonality of our brokenness, sins, needs, and trials to reach people all over the world with His good news of salvation.

This is because we have all faced the deep, piercing pain of losing someone we care for through betrayal, distance, rejection, or death. We also realize how wonderful it is to be loved and to cherish others in return. And whether we recognize it or not, we long to be accepted, to belong, and to be considered worthy—especially by the One who comprehends us completely and will never forsake us.

This is why our strongest, most long-lasting relationships are usually with individuals we trust enough to share our most intimate thoughts and feelings with. We feel joined to them because they appreciate and comprehend us, which is often due to the fact that they've experienced many of the same trials, emotions, and comforts from the Father as we have.

Unfortunately, we often use our emotions as an excuse to build walls in opposition to each other. Someone offends, upsets, or stirs the envy within us and how do we react? Rather than seeking to comprehend where they are coming from or why they bring up these pains within us, we write them off, bad-mouth them, and try to turn others against them.

But there is a reason God calls us to "Rejoice with those who rejoice, and weep with those who weep. . . . If possible, so far as it depends on you, be at peace with all men" (Rom. 12:15, 18). He gave us our emotions to understand one another—so we could reach into another's deepest wounds and become His instrument of healing to them (2 Cor. 1:3–7).

God gave us our emotions to understand one another—so we could reach into another's deepest wounds and become His instrument of healing to them.

This is one of the reasons Jesus came to Earth. Of course, the most important purpose was to reconcile us to the Father through the cross. But Hebrews 2:17–18 also tells us Christ "had to be made like His brethren in all things, so that He might become a merciful and faithful high priest in things pertaining to God, to make propitiation for the sins of the people. For since He Himself was tempted in that which He has suffered, He is able to come to the aid of those who are tempted."

Our Savior wanted to know how we feel, so He could relate

to us in a meaningful way and truly help us live. He wanted to connect with us so we could unite with Him and experience the profound, abiding joy of knowing the Lord. We are called to do likewise with others.

3. So We Can Reflect the Image of God

Galatians 5:22–23 tells us, "The fruit of the Spirit is love, joy, peace, patience, kindness, goodness, faithfulness, gentleness, [and] self-control." This means that when the character of Christ is formed in us through the work of the Holy Spirit, these are the qualities that flow out from us (Rom. 8:29). The Father does this so we can demonstrate His graciousness, mercy, and passion to the world. These were never meant to be passive virtues that merely make us feel better about ourselves. Rather, the Lord gave us these Spirit-born feelings to mobilize us to action.

For example, consider the godly attribute of kindness. It isn't formed within us so that others will know us as nice people—though that may be a by-product. What the Father really wants is to stir His emotion of compassion within us so we will faithfully express it to others. The apostle James asks, "If a brother or sister is without clothing and in need of daily food, and one of you says to them, 'Go in peace, be warmed and be filled,' and yet you do not give them what is necessary for their body, what use is that?" (James 2:15–16). In other words, we need to actively demonstrate kindness.

Why? Because as we do so, God works through us to draw others to Himself. This is in accordance with Jesus' command in

Matthew 5:16, in which He tells us, "Let your light shine before men in such a way that they may see your good works, and glorify your Father who is in heaven."

Therefore, through our emotions, the Lord marshals us to do His kingdom work and to fulfill His plans in the world. Or, as Paul says in 2 Corinthians 5:20, "We are ambassadors for Christ, as though God were making an appeal through us." We reflect His character and love so others can know Him and experience His mercy.

This means He will work through your emotions to help you understand His purpose for your life. For example, what stirs compassion in your heart? What injustices make you especially angry? Who is it that you cannot bear to see suffering? The Lord may have given you a special sensitivity in your heart for that person or group of people so you could be a blessing to them.

> *God will work through your emotions to help you understand His purpose for your life.*

SOMETHING'S WRONG

Now, we know that the Father gave us our emotions so we could enjoy life, relate to others, and represent Him in the world. Also, in 2 Timothy 1:7, the apostle Paul assures us, "God has not given us a spirit of fear, but of power and of love and of a sound mind" (NKJV). So why is it that so many struggle with anxiety, rejection, bitterness, guilt, and despair? Why do we get stuck when dealing with these feelings and how do they gain such overwhelming strength in our lives?

As we noted previously, this happens when we lack control over this powerful force within us. Our emotions were given to serve us, but they become liabilities when they are not under our command. This is due to the fact many people try to manage their feelings in unhealthy ways that are not at all helpful.

1. The Belief That Emotion Is a Weakness

Some believe that being emotional is a sign of weakness—that men should not cry and so forth—so they repress what they feel. Of course, we know that is not true because the Lord Jesus wept (John 11:35) and often expressed His joy (Luke 10:21), anger (Matt. 21:12–13), and other sentiments. But these individuals refuse to acknowledge that they experience certain emotions at all. They deny their feelings, continually rejecting the fact that they exist. So their distresses and grievances remain trapped within them—wreaking havoc on their lives, health, and relationships.

2. The Inclination to Suppress or Stifle Emotions

Some people recognize that they have feelings—they admit they are present—but refuse to express them. This could be for all sorts of reasons. Perhaps they fear what they sense within themselves or do not know how to communicate their sentiments in a healthy manner. It could be that they were taught at a young age that emotions are their enemies—to reveal what they are feeling is to give power to others. Whatever the cause, they, like those who repress their concerns, keep their hurts trapped within them and experience pain and isolation. They may also seek to vent their frustrations in covert, devious, or vindictive ways, but it never helps.

3. The Drive to Drown Out Emotions

People who do this feel and express their emotions, but attempt to dull their effects through any number of means—busyness, hobbies, mood-altering substances, addictive behaviors, unhealthy relationships, etc. Perhaps they believe if they numb their feelings sufficiently, their wounds will eventually heal by themselves. Or maybe they are simply trying to escape long enough for the most excruciating of the hurts to subside. Sadly, when a person does not address his or her pain, it never really goes away. It simply festers within them, causing other problems.

4. The Need to Express All Emotions Without a Filter

The fourth error people make in responding to their emotions is to express everything they feel all of the time with barely any filter. This, of course, is never wise. Look at what the book of Proverbs has to say about unrestraint:

- "When there are many words, transgression is unavoidable, but he who restrains his lips is wise." (10:19)
- "A quick-tempered man acts foolishly." (14:17)

- "Like a city that is broken into and without walls is a man who has no control over his spirit." (25:27–28)
- "A fool always loses his temper, but a wise man holds it back." (29:11)
- "An angry man stirs up strife, and a hot-tempered man abounds in transgression." (29:22)

Unwise, indeed. These individuals often vent their emotions without any discipline or discretion—and they do so to anyone who has the misfortune of being around them. They may even find this to be an effective way to get attention. But instead of alleviating their suffering, this actually serves to deepen and intensify it.

This is not to say we don't need an outlet for our feelings. We absolutely do. We all benefit from loving, godly people who will listen to us and give us wise counsel. But even our closest, most devoted friends do not want to know all the complaints we have, every time we have them. They could not bear that, and we should not ask them to.

Instead, if you would like a truly safe and restorative place to express your emotions, there is only One who offers that—and that is the Father.

Here is what you can do: Go to your bedroom, your prayer closet, or wherever you can have some time alone. It is best if no one will interrupt you. Get on your knees, open the Word of God, and tell the Lord whatever you're feeling. Be

Get on your knees, open the Word of God, and tell the Lord whatever you're feeling.

honest—He will not get mad at you. In fact, He already knows what you are thinking and what's plaguing you.

Not only is He always willing to listen, but when you are in such pain that you cannot communicate what's in your heart, He also assures you of help. "The Spirit also helps our weakness; for we do not know how to pray as we should, but the Spirit Himself intercedes for us with groanings too deep for words; and He who searches the hearts knows what the mind of the Spirit is, because He intercedes for the saints according to the will of God" (Rom. 8:26–27). This is a particularly important promise if you are used to repressing or suppressing your emotions. It may be that you do not understand what you feel or have never learned how to articulate what's inside of you. The Holy Spirit can teach you the healthy, beneficial ways to express and take hold of your emotions.

FINDING THE REAL ROOT

Of course, I am certain there are those who wonder, *What about counseling? Medication? Group therapy? Aren't those needed? Don't some people need extra help for their problems?*

Yes, some do—and God can work through those remedies to help people. However, there are so many who have tried everything and still haven't found rest from their painful emotions or any victory in their lives. Nothing seems to reach deep enough within them. Therefore, my goal as a pastor and fellow believer is to help with the spiritual aspect of your feelings, because that truly permeates everything else in your life.

Unfortunately, in our find-it-fast world, our first response is often to seek a solution that covers the wounds we have, rather than really healing them.

For instance, we know medication is necessary for those who have true biochemical imbalances. When our bodies are not functioning as they should, the physical problems can affect our emotions. A good example of this is an underactive thyroid (also known as *hypothyroidism*), which can slow a person down, making the individual feel weary, drained, and depressed. Conversely, an overactive thyroid (also known as *hyperthyroidism*) can increase a person's level of irritability and anxiety. Both of these conditions—and the others that cause an imbalance of your internal chemistry—can and should be treated.

However, it concerns me greatly how often people turn to prescription treatments—often enduring the most terrible side effects imaginable—merely to *numb* their emotions. The problems still exist because they are not truly biochemical or physical in nature; rather, they are relational and spiritual.

I realize that as you read this, it is possible you've already made this choice; perhaps you have turned to medications to anesthetize your anguish but are still struggling. My prayer is that you will realize that God has better plans for you and He wants you to be free. The Father can heal the emotional bondage that remains within you that no prescription has been able to or will ever be able to touch. Of course, this

The Father can heal the emotional bondage that remains within you that no medication has been able to or will ever be able to touch.

does not mean you should discontinue using a medication immediately without your doctor's guidance—some drugs have devastating effects if stopped too quickly. Rather, what I am saying is that if your problem is not biochemical or physical, there is a far better and more effective way to deal with it—and that is with God's help. The Lord can give you victory over the pain you feel. You do not have to live with a dulled version of those emotions constantly assailing you.

As for Christian counselors, I think they can be extremely helpful as long as you're careful. You should always be cautious about whose advice you listen to and put into practice. Therefore, when looking for a counselor, the wisest thing to do is make sure the person you speak with is not only a mature believer who is focused on God but also a faithful confidant who will also be discreet about what you share with him.

Christian counselors can be very effective in helping us overcome difficult emotions. They can teach us a great deal about why we respond the way we do. They can also show us the important tools we need in order to overcome our difficulties. In fact, I think the most important benefit we can gain from godly counselors, mentors, and leaders is their helping us identify the patterns of thinking that are keeping us in bondage.

Our emotions are the product of our thought-life.

You see, our feelings really find their root in the beliefs we focus on and the messages we repeat to ourselves. Our emotions are the product of our thought-life.

Proverbs 23:7 tells us that as a person "thinks within himself, so he is." If we continually tell ourselves, "I am worthless. I am inadequate. No one respects me. No one could ever love me," it is no wonder that our emotions are a devastating mess. This affects everything about us—our health, relationships, and even how our faces appear to others.

This is why Paul tells us, "Do not be conformed to this world, but be transformed by the renewing of your mind" (Rom. 12:2). He understood that our feelings and behavior could only change when the Holy Spirit's transformational work had begun in our minds.

This is the reason it is so exceedingly important to spend time in God's Word and in His powerful presence. We need to take hold of what the Lord—the limitless Creator of heaven and earth, our wise Maker, faithful Savior, omnipotent Defender, loving heavenly Father, and sovereign King—has to say about us, rather than believing the lies we've been told by flawed and fallen humanity.

I have seen this firsthand throughout the years, but especially as I preached a series of sermons entitled, "How the Truth Can Set You Free" based on John 8:32, "You will know the truth, and the truth will make you free." Every week, invariably someone would approach me, their face radiant, their new freedom shining in their eyes, and would say, "Dr. Stanley, the Lord has really set me free—He has changed my life through His truth. Thank you for teaching me!"

I can recall thinking, *Father, I am grateful You're doing this awesome work . . . but what about me? I want to experience that freedom as well.*

I knew I wasn't living with the abundant joy and liberty He had given me. Thankfully, after months of seeing people transformed by His Word, God finally changed me, too. I learned that, by faith, my thinking had to be revolutionized. I had to give up what I believed and take His truth as absolute, undeniable, unchangeable, unwavering fact.

> *I had to give up what I believed and take His truth as absolute, undeniable, unchangeable, unwavering fact.*

This is my prayer for you as well. You see, somewhere along the line, there are falsehoods that have gotten stuck in your thought patterns. There are lies that you repeat to yourself as you make decisions about your circumstances. For you to be free, those have to be removed and replaced with the powerful principles of the everlasting God.

Are you willing? It will take some work—disciplined biblical reflection and faithful obedience to the Savior—but I guarantee it is worth it. Because "if the Son makes you free, you will be free indeed" (John 8:36). And isn't that what you truly long for, after all?

‖‖‖

Father, thank You for the gift of emotions. How grateful I am that through them I can enjoy and appreciate the life You've given me, I can relate to others in a meaningful way, and I can reflect Your image to this hurting world. In faith I claim that my emotions are a blessing from You and that

You can work through them for my good and Your glory.

Lord God, I confess that at times I have allowed my negative feelings and false beliefs to rule me—allowing them to stand in direct opposition to what You are doing in and through me. You promise that when we repent of our sins, You are faithful and just to forgive our sins and cleanse us from all unrighteousness. So I thank You, Father, both for forgiving me and for teaching me how to be free from the lies that keep me in bondage.

Help me to be completely honest about how I feel and the struggles I have. Where I am repressing or suppressing emotions, please unearth them and show me how to verbalize what I feel to You. Where I have drowned my feelings and tried to escape them, please give me courage to bravely confront them. And whenever I am tempted to complain to a friend or grumble about something I am experiencing, please remind me to take my concerns to You first. Open Your Word to me, guide me in Your truth, and help me to be obedient to You in every situation that may arise.

Thank You, Father, for hearing my prayers and beginning the process of transforming the way I think. Thank You for setting me free with Your truth and teaching me the boundaries that protect me and honor You. To You alone belong all glory, power, and praise in abundance. In Jesus' name I pray. Amen.

QUESTIONS FOR
PERSONAL REFLECTION AND GROUP STUDY

1. What makes your emotions gifts from God?

2. Of the reasons given for why the Lord gave us the ability to feel, which one(s) do you relate to the most? Why is this aspect important to you?

3. Have your emotions ever kept you from obeying God's call? Explain the circumstances.

4. Are you more apt to express your feelings or suppress them? How has that method affected your relationships with others?

5. How could opening yourself emotionally to the Father help give you a sense of freedom in your relationship with Him?

6. Has God moved you to a better understanding of your emotions and thoughts through this material so far? How so?

7. Have you ever experienced God's leading in terms of understanding the plans He has for your life? If so, how did it make you feel? If not, what do you think is preventing you from knowing the Lord's will?

3

THE ROOT OF ALL
PAINFUL EMOTIONS

Identifying the Original Source
of Our Woundedness

NOTHING IS MORE SATISFYING TO me than experiencing the presence of God in the great outdoors. I love seeing and photographing the magnificent grandeur of His creation as it spreads out before me—mountains and valleys, deserts and buttes, oceans and beaches—all revealing a different aspect of His imaginative power. I also enjoy sitting by a roaring campfire at night and fellowshipping with friends, riding horseback on isolated highland trails, and exploring remote roads through forests or along rugged coastlines.

But as much as I delight in these activities, I have absolutely no desire to encounter a rattlesnake or grizzly bear in the wilderness—or any other kind of dangerous animal for that matter. As you can imagine, I have a healthy respect for these amazing creatures. And since I cannot outrun or outswim them, I think it best not to get too close.

I imagine that at least part of my reluctance to approach these predatory beasts stems from one of the most terrifying experiences of my life. I was camping in a remote area high atop the Canadian Rockies, where some friends and I were taking photographs. The scenery was absolutely magnificent. After a very satisfying day of capturing incredible images and breathing in the crisp mountain air, we retreated to our respective tents for a good night of slumber.

I was awakened suddenly out of a profound sleep. My tent was moving about violently in a way I had never experienced before—so much so that even in the deep dark of night I could sense its forceful reeling. The thought raced through my mind: *What could possibly be shaking my tent like this?*

Instantly, a shock wave of fear shot through me, putting my entire body into near paralysis. I didn't hear any sounds other than the wind in the trees, but I had absolutely no doubt that there could only be one thing in the world that could make such a commotion.

It had to be a bear.

My heart racing, I held my breath. I knew that in a moment, I would see its long, terrible claws rip apart the tent above my head and then I would be face-to-face with an angry grizzly. I was sure of it.

What did I do? Nothing. I couldn't move. I couldn't open my mouth. I couldn't do a thing except think about the intense pain that was ahead. I waited in terror.

After what seemed to be a very long time, the movement of the tent subsided. I wondered if the bear had given up on my tent and chosen to attack one of my companions. I strained my ears, listening for growling or other grizzly noises. I still couldn't hear anything—no snarling, rumbling, or even breathing. The grip of fear began to dissipate slowly. After a few minutes, I decided to take a cautious look outside.

The only thing I saw was . . . snow? No bears—just a thick white blanket covering the ground and most of my tent, where there had been none before. And there was a lot of it.

By that time, my camping companions were also venturing a peek outside their tents. We looked at one another and at the transformed surroundings in bewilderment. Finally we realized what had happened and began chuckling at how foolish we had been. What we'd thought was a bear attack was just a simple snowstorm! We laughed until our sides ached.

Was I afraid for my life in those few minutes? Absolutely. My friends were as well. But I tell you this story to illustrate the terrible power fear can have over us. The anxieties we experience don't need to be rooted in reality. They can paralyze us simply through what we *perceive* to be a threat.

And even when we are able to laugh about the situations that first caused us to panic, hidden scars are often left behind, tainting how we view our circumstances. In an instant, our fear can set patterns in our thinking that are difficult to identify and challenging to root out but that affect the course of our lives nonetheless.

> *In an instant, our fear can set patterns in our thinking that are difficult to identify and challenging to root out.*

The good news is that the God who defeated sin and death

is able to dislodge the fearful thoughts and beliefs from within us. He says, "Do not fear, for I am with you; do not anxiously look about you, for I am your God. I will strengthen you, surely I will help you, surely I will uphold you with My righteous right hand" (Isa. 41:10). Understanding His mighty presence with us is the key to overcoming whatever scares us. We discover that with Him providing for and protecting us, there's really no need to be frightened at all.

STARTING WITH FEAR

Of course you may be wondering why I begin with the emotion of fear when there are so many others. It is because I believe that the origin of every other negative response we face is some kind of anxiety. After all, fear is an uneasy feeling of dread—like an alarm that goes off inside of us, warning us that something bad is going to happen. It can be caused by a perceived threat or can occur when we lose control in a particular situation.

When this apprehension persists over a long period of time, we subconsciously build up defenses around those weaknesses or vulnerable areas. And the safeguards we construct, unfortunately, cause other problems to arise.

For example, if as children we experienced times when there wasn't enough money to buy the necessities of life or we faced times of deprivation, we may have an ingrained fear of going hungry that drives us. So we attempt to safeguard ourselves by attaining possessions, which we believe will protect us from starvation.

But as we grow, something happens within us. Eventually, our motivation is not just focused on putting food on the table and fulfilling basic needs, but about amassing material goods in order to satisfy our desires for significance and achievement—the deeper hungers of our soul. The wealth we acquire becomes our security, identity, and sole goal in life. Before we know it, our lives are defined by greed and are empty of the meaning God has for us. The fear of going hungry is still there, buried far beneath destructive layers of our own defenses, continually driving us in the wrong direction.

Of course, this is a rather simplistic explanation of how a fear can form the basis of our other painful feelings, but you can see how it can occur. And it illustrates an important principle: When we think about the adverse emotions we experience in specific areas of our lives—such as finances, relationships, and concerns about the future—and we examine their deepest roots, *most often we find that anxiety forms the foundation of those destructive feelings.* For example:

- As we saw, *greed* is based on the fear of not having or being enough or of missing out on something important.
- *Rejection* and *loneliness* are both rooted in the concern that we will not be accepted—that we will be abandoned or forsaken.
- *Guilt* is apprehension that our sinful behavior and wrongdoing will be discovered or that we will be punished.

- *Pride* is founded on the trepidation that we will be found unworthy or incapable.
- *Discouragement* is a fear that hope is lost or that failure is the only possible outcome, and it is caused by a lack of confidence or a sense of inadequacy.
- *Despair* is based on worries of what's occurred in the past or what might happen and how our losses, experiences, feelings of unworthiness, and mistakes impact our future.
- *Jealousy* is the dread that we will lose what we desire or that we will not measure up when compared to others.
- *Anger* is caused by the apprehension that we may not get our way, are being treated disrespectfully, or that someone who has wronged us will not be chastised adequately.
- *Indecision* is the paralysis caused when we worry that we will make the wrong choice.

Do you struggle with any of these? Can you see how fear is the basis of the negative emotions we all feel? So much of the agony we experience in life is caused by our anxieties. It is the enemy's most effective tool for tempting us to sin, prolonging our bondage, and keeping us separated from God.

As we saw in the first chapter, one of the first emotions mentioned in the Bible is fear. I believe that it was not only the result of the fall but also how the serpent was able to influence Eve. Look at the biblical account:

The serpent . . . said to the woman, "Indeed, has God said, 'You shall not eat from any tree of the garden'?" The woman said to the serpent, "From the fruit of the trees of the garden we may eat; but from the fruit of the tree which is in the middle of the garden, God has said, 'You shall not eat from it or touch it, or you will die.'" The serpent said to the woman, "You surely will not die! For God knows that in the day you eat from it your eyes will be opened, and you will be like God, knowing good and evil." When the woman saw that the tree was good for food, and that it was a delight to the eyes, and that the tree was desirable to make one wise, she took from its fruit and ate; and she gave also to her husband with her, and he ate. (Gen. 3:1–6)

How did the serpent use fear to tempt Eve? By planting the seed of doubt in her mind about the Lord's intentions and character. There had to have been questions that arose in her mind after that interaction. Perhaps she wondered, *Could it be that God is really keeping something from me? Why wouldn't He want me to be like Him—knowing good and evil? This tree looks fine, it doesn't make sense that I can't have some of this fruit. What is He hiding from me?*

The result was that Eve began to distrust the Father's command and feared missing out on becoming "like God" (Gen. 3:5). So she reached out and took fruit from the only tree in the entire garden that was forbidden to her.

The same happens to us. After all, aren't those some of the questions we ask? *Why did the Lord allow this to happen to me?*

Why isn't He giving me the desires of my heart? Will I ever get what I want? We're worried we won't receive what we yearn for, so we rush ahead and take it for ourselves. And like Adam and Eve, we find ourselves even worse off—wounded, separated from the true desire of our hearts, and with deeper grief than we could have imagined.

As we saw previously, when God walked through the garden after the fall and called for Adam and Eve, they hid from Him because they were afraid of how He would react to their disobedience, lack of covering, and broken relationship. Recall how Adam replied: "I heard the sound of You in the garden, and I was afraid because I was naked; so I hid myself" (Gen. 3:10).

Had the Father ever given Adam and Eve any reason to distrust Him? No. He had not even addressed their rebellion at that point. But it was that deep sense of being exposed and found lacking that was at the root of their fears.

> *It is a deep sense of being exposed and found lacking that is at the root of our fears.*

It's at the core of our anxieties as well. From that time forward, most of mankind has avoided intimacy with God because, frankly, He knows how flawed, rebellious, and inadequate we are. We feel vulnerable—embarrassed to walk with Him. We are frightened that He will reject us, punish us, or reveal the things we despise most about ourselves to others.

This is one of the reasons the majority of religions are based on works. People can feel good about themselves by conforming to rituals that never reveal their true inner feelings or brokenness—that never require them to get close to the Lord. There is no power in those religions, but there is also no danger of being exposed. Sadly, there's no salvation either.

The only faith founded on a relationship is Christianity. We're promised, "Draw near to God and He will draw near to you" (James 4:8). Yes, this means we open our hearts to the Father, who knows everything about us. Our sins are uncovered, our anxieties are revealed, and our faults are open to His view. But we can trust the Lord with the deep places of hurt within us. Remember, "He heals the brokenhearted and binds up their wounds" (Ps. 147:3). This is where true restoration can occur. He shows us the healthy way to overcome all that hinders us.

The first thing you must deal with in healing your emotions is confronting any reservation you have to being completely open, honest, and personal with God.

This is why we are beginning with fear. Because the first thing you must deal with in healing your emotions is confronting any reservation you have to being completely open, honest, and personal with God.

IN AWE OF GOD

But perhaps this is a bit confusing. Maybe you're wondering, *Doesn't the Bible tell us to fear God?* Yes, it does. In fact it says, "The fear of the LORD is the beginning of wisdom, and the knowledge of the Holy One is understanding" (Prov. 9:10). However, what the Bible depicts is not terror in approaching Him. It does not mean we should avoid spending time with Him or hide away from Him as Adam and Eve did.

On the contrary, what Scripture tells us is that we should *respect* what God says, honoring Him by obeying His leadership. We should acknowledge that He is the highest authority with the greatest wisdom and power. And we should submit to Him because He is a holy God—His instructions to us are good, He is in control, and He has never broken a promise.

You do not have to be afraid of being close to your heavenly Father. Quite the opposite! It is the highest honor and privilege you and I are ever given. We should be motivated to enjoy His presence and fellowship.

So let me ask you: Are you enjoying a regular, consistent time alone with the Father? Do you go before Him daily in prayer, listening for His direction? Or do you simply pray whenever there is an emergency?

Take an honest inventory of your true attitude toward God. Perhaps you would say, "Well, I don't have much time for prayer." I hear this often, but it is usually just an excuse hiding deeper issues. If you really see the Lord as your loving and omnipotent Creator, King, and Redeemer—the sovereign God who will lead you to success in every endeavor—you will want to spend time with Him and trust the plans He has for you. But if you see Him as a disinterested force out yonder or a cruel deity who is looking forward to punishing you, it is no wonder you're not compelled to be near Him.

If you don't feel inspired to experience the Lord's presence, examine why that is. What is the source of your reticence to approach Him? Your perception of Him may be inaccurate—formed by negative experiences with earthly authority figures instead of His truth. You must overcome this, because the path to healing for every damaged emotion begins with a relationship with Him. Therefore, I urge you to take a moment to pray:

Father, how grateful I am for Your love and grace. Thank You for revealing the wounds within me and the profound roots of anxieties that are keeping me in bondage. I ask that You would not only reveal them to me, but teach me to overcome them, even right now.

Lord, it is possible that some of these apprehensions came from authority figures early in my life who tainted how I view You. Father, I want to know who You are—who You've shown Yourself to be in Your Word and throughout history. Drive out any wrong understanding I have of Your character or intentions. Help me to see Your face. Tear down my defenses and become my only security, identity, and the highest goal of my life. I know that when I trust in You, I will never be disappointed.

Thank You, Father, that Your healing in me has begun. Continue to draw me to You. Through Your Holy Spirit reveal what is hidden, restore what has been damaged, and make me into everything You dreamed I could be when You created me. In Jesus' name I pray. Amen.

EVERYTHING TO GAIN

You may not believe this at the moment, but whenever you express to the Father your desires for healing, you take an enormous step in the right direction. God is always talking to you—continually calling to you about the wonderful plans He has for your life. You and I do not always hear what the Lord has to say because we're not focused on Him. But once you turn to God and begin listening to Him, He starts revealing the inner workings of your heart and initiates the healing process. He does so by sending you circumstances that expose your area of anxiety and helping you work through them—mending the brokenness in you by teaching you His truth.

This is why prayer is so important to the process of healing your emotions and why I will often encourage you to seek the Father. You *need* time with God. Whether you realize it or not, your very soul is hungry for His presence. Your spirit requires deep, meaningful, intimate communion with Him—even more than your body needs food and water. He can satisfy, strengthen, and calm your fears in a manner none other can. And as you discover His character and His ways—that He is truly sovereign, wise, and caring—you learn to trust Him more and are able to accept what He is teaching you in increasing measure.

Your spirit requires deep, meaningful, intimate communion with God—even more than your body needs food and water.

This is why David testifies, "O LORD, You have searched me

and known me. You know when I sit down and when I rise up; You understand my thought from afar. You scrutinize my path and my lying down, and are intimately acquainted with all my ways. . . . Search me, O God, and know my heart; try me and know my anxious thoughts; and see if there be any hurtful way in me, and lead me in the everlasting way" (Ps. 139:1–3, 23–24). After years of relying upon God, David realized that the Lord knew him better than he knew himself. So he invited the Father to release him from the hidden burdens that kept him in distress with full confidence in His wisdom, love, and power.

Likewise, you don't need to know what to heal because God will teach you how to be free. He knows you completely—down to the smallest and most intimate detail—and He understands what must change within you. He also recognizes the most effective way to liberate you from your fears and other areas of bondage.

You can trust Him. So take a leap of faith into the arms of your loving Father and stop hiding. Allow Him to strip away the destructive coping mechanisms, hidden scars, and layers of paralyzing anxiety. Spend time with Him. Cast "all your anxiety on Him, because He cares for you" (1 Pet. 5:7). You have nothing to fear, but everything to gain.

Father, how grateful I am that You will not allow me to remain in bondage, but bring my anxieties to light so that I can be free of them. I bless and praise You for Your kindness to me and the patience with which You heal my wounds.

Lord, I bring all my fears to You—both the ones that are obvious and the ones that are hidden within my heart. You know how deeply they consume me and dominate my thoughts. I cannot break free of these apprehensions on my own. But, Lord, I commit them to Your loving care and faithful stewardship, knowing You have never let me down and never will. I want to trust You more—to find rest in Your faithfulness and provision. Help me to let down my defenses. Exposing my vulnerabilities, failures, and fears may be difficult, but I know that is the only way to truly know You and be free.

Thank You for being my Father, understanding my situation, and caring for me enough to help me. I am so grateful that You love me unconditionally, have promised to provide for me, and have the wisdom and strength necessary to break me free of this bondage.

Lord, I acknowledge that what I am facing is a faith battle and that it comes down to what I really believe about You. Therefore, I declare once and for all that I trust You. I believe You can deliver me from this anxiety, Father—that You are bigger, stronger, and more powerful than any problem I could face. I don't want the enemy to keep me from knowing You any longer through fear. Drive out any stronghold he has constructed. I give my life to You, Lord God, and I have faith that You will always do what is absolutely best.

Thank You for revealing my wounds and helping me heal. In Jesus' name I pray. Amen.

QUESTIONS FOR
PERSONAL REFLECTION AND GROUP STUDY

1. What is the most frightening experience you've ever had? How did you initially deal with your fear? Does it still cause you anxiety when you think about it? Why do you think this is?

2. What were you most afraid of as a child? Is there any evidence those fears still exist in your life? How have your anxieties changed throughout the years?

3. Which form of anxiety do you struggle with most often today?

4. What types of questions or messages run through your mind when you're facing a fearful situation or anxious circumstances?

5. How difficult is it for you to be completely open and honest about your true emotions with God?

6. What reservations do you have when it comes to revealing your innermost fears, concerns, and questions as you communicate with your heavenly Father?

4

REVIEWING THE EVIDENCE

Recognizing Ingrained Fear by Examining the Consequences

I ONCE KNEW A YOUNG man who regularly watched the *In Touch* television program with his grandmother. They lived in Atlanta, but whenever he would ask her to visit First Baptist with him, she would respond the same way, "I'm sorry son, I don't like big churches. Let's just watch the broadcast."

"Why don't you like large churches, Grandma?" he would ask.

"I just don't," she would reply firmly, in a tone that warned him further discussion would not be appreciated.

As you can imagine, this confused the young man quite a bit. He couldn't understand why his grandmother would dismiss a church without ever going to see it—especially since they were blessed by the messages on the program each week. He felt a deep conviction that it was important for both of them to fellowship with other believers. So he continued asking her to accompany him to church until she finally agreed to go.

I'm happy to tell you that she loved it. In fact, she joined the First Baptist Atlanta family the very next week.

But I was intrigued by what had hindered her from visiting in the first place. Did she really dislike big churches? Had she been hurt by a congregation somewhere? No. She later told me she just always *thought* she would be averse to such a setting, but she never understood why. I asked her several questions to see if I could get to the heart of why a large church had been so off-putting to her.

Finally, she replied, "I guess somewhere inside of me I just thought, *It's too big. No one will even notice me. No one will be kind to me or care about me.* I figured there was no use in visiting." In other words, she was afraid people would be unfriendly and reject her. But when she stepped through the doors of First Baptist Atlanta, the reality was far different from what she had imagined. Many people greeted her, welcomed her with a warm handshake or hug, and showed a genuine interest in her. She instantly felt loved and accepted.

Her subconscious, undefined fears almost prevented her from experiencing the great blessing of having a devoted church family. The same thing can happen to us in different areas of our lives if we never confront why we think and react as we do in certain situations. As I explained previously, we may have underlying currents of anxiety influencing our decisions and perceptions without even knowing it. This is why it is so important that we identify what we're actually telling ourselves.

VALID FEAR

But perhaps you are still reticent to admit that you have any anxiety in your life. Or maybe you are not fully convinced that your worries are all that bad. After all, isn't it natural and reasonable to have some concerns—especially in this volatile and ever-changing world?

Fear of God Is Good and Essential

As we saw in the previous chapter, it is not just good, but absolutely essential that we fear the Lord. So, it is true that not all fear is negative. It is right for us to show reverence to God for who He is—our sovereign King, wise Counselor, and loving Leader. In Psalm 34:9–15, David affirms:

> O fear the LORD, you His saints; for to those who fear Him there is no want. The young lions do lack and suffer hunger; but they who seek the LORD shall not be in want of any good thing. Come, you children, listen to me; I will teach you the fear of the LORD. Who is the man who desires life and loves length of days that he may see good? Keep your tongue from evil and your lips from speaking deceit. Depart from evil and do good; seek peace and pursue it. The eyes of the LORD are toward the righteous and His ears are open to their cry. (Ps. 34:9–15)

Our obedience to the Lord and respect for His ways always bring us blessings. Why? Because God assumes full responsibility for our needs and covers us with His umbrella of protection when we submit to Him. Our circumstances may not always be pleasant or easy—in fact, at times they may be very difficult. But we are assured, "The angel of the LORD encamps around those who fear Him, and rescues them" (Ps. 34:7). Therefore, honor and revere the Father above everything else.

Uneasiness Can Be a Valuable Alert

There are also times when our uneasiness in a situation serves as an important red flag, alerting us to a possibility that harm could befall us. As I said before, it is good to have a healthy caution when approaching dangerous predators or potentially explosive situations—such as an active volcano.

I recall when the long-dormant Mount St. Helens in Washington began to rumble, causing thousands of earthquakes throughout March and April of 1980. By April 29, officials had closed off the area to the public due to the increasingly imminent threat caused by the massive pressure building in its core.

Sadly, many refused to heed their warnings. When it finally erupted on May 18, 1980, fifty-seven people lost their lives, though they had plenty of time to evacuate. In that instance, a sense of uneasiness and concern over the looming danger would have served them well.

Knowledge That Sin Has Perilous Consequences

It takes wisdom to realize the dangerous consequences of sin and to avoid it. What is sin? It is when we willfully choose our way rather than God's. We attempt to meet our needs or accomplish our goals in our own way, despite what He tells us in His Word. Yet Galatians 6:7–8 solemnly cautions us, "Do not be deceived, God is not mocked; for whatever a man sows, this he will also reap. For the one who sows to his own flesh will from the flesh reap corruption, but the one who sows to the Spirit will from the Spirit reap eternal life."

Of course, if you are a believer, you are no longer in danger of eternal separation from God. However, you still bear the devastating consequences of your sinful behaviors, including all of the emotional, relational, and/or financial problems that accompany them. If you steal or kill, you will still be responsible for breaking the laws of the land. If you are deceptive in your dealings with others, your character will be marked and people won't trust you. Sinful actions produce painful results. Therefore, you are wise to flee whenever you are tempted to sin.

Shock Relating to Disturbing Facts

A fourth way we experience valid fear is directly after we receive a disturbing report or face a shocking situation. When we are blindsided by unexpected news—perhaps we receive word that a loved one has been in an accident or has a precarious medical condition—anxiety is a natural reaction. The immediate concern we feel often compels us to take appropriate action. We seek more information, wise counsel, and the best way to respond to whatever challenges are ahead of us.

Likewise, if we are attacked in some way or we run into something unexpected—like a rattlesnake or grizzly bear on a hike—our adrenaline level can spike quickly, initiating our fight-or-flight response and preparing us for the encounter almost instantaneously.

WHEN ANXIETY CONTINUES

We can see there are some perfectly acceptable grounds for feeling fear, and there are likely more than I have listed here. In fact, I sometimes experience a sense of unease and restlessness when God is about to move me in a new direction. This is the way He gets my attention so I do not miss what He is telling me. Some feelings of apprehension are legitimate and even useful.

However, I find that these aren't the anxieties people usually complain about. Rather, their reasons are generally much more long-term and profound. People are intensely worried about their jobs, families, finances, health, world politics, unmet desires, and even how they measure up to other's expectations.

For example, not long ago a friend and I were chatting and he said, "I just went to see my financial advisor—we sat down and made some projections about my retirement. Since I'm over seventy now, I wanted to make sure everything is okay and that I have enough in my portfolio to live out the rest of my life. But I have to tell you, Charles, I came away more unsure about my future than ever. The more I think about what the days ahead may hold, the more jittery I become."

Another person confided, "My doctor told me the condition I have is getting worse—it's developing into something that may not be curable. He doesn't know of any way to treat this particular disease or to impede it from progressing. I feel like jelly inside. This is it—my health is deteriorating and I can't do anything about it."

Countless people, like the two above, have very serious problems to deal with. Sadly, instead of turning their attention to God's provision, many of the people I meet choose to fret continually about their troubles—they remain uneasy about the future and are unable to think about anything other than the difficult challenges before them. Their fears are overpowering, affect other areas of their lives, and often feel absolutely insurmountable. Consequently, their incessant focus on their problems makes them feel as if their lives will never improve.

Incessant focus on problems makes us feel as if our lives will never improve.

Maybe this sounds familiar to you. Perhaps you are experiencing something very similar. Let me assure you: the continual nervousness you feel is not from the Father. The Lord never intended for you to endure a relentless onslaught of anxiety, which is what far too many of us do. That's not how God wants you or anyone to live.

This is why Jesus instructed the following:

Do not be worried about your life, as to what you will eat or what you will drink; nor for your body, as to what you will put on. Is not life more than food, and the body more than clothing? Look at the birds of the air, that they do not sow, nor reap nor gather into barns, and yet your heavenly Father feeds them. Are you not worth much more than they?

And who of you by being worried can add a single hour to his life? And why are you worried about clothing? Observe how the lilies of the field grow; they do not toil nor do they spin, yet I say to you that not even Solomon in all his glory clothed himself like one of these. But if God so clothes the grass of the field, which is alive today and tomorrow is thrown into the furnace, will He not much more clothe you? You of little faith!

Do not worry then, saying, 'What will we eat?' or 'What will we drink?' or 'What will we wear for clothing?' For the Gentiles eagerly seek all these things; for your heavenly Father knows that you need all these things. But seek first His kingdom and His righteousness, and all these things will be added to you. So do not worry about tomorrow; for tomorrow will care for itself. Each day has enough trouble of its own. (Matt. 6:25–34)

Jesus did not deny that anxiety exists. There are many things in the world that can cause us to become frightened. But He pointed out two significant truths that are important for us to note:

1. Our fears do not achieve us anything of value.
2. Our focus should be on our Father, who faithfully provides.

In other words, we need to look past our problems and center our attention on our all-powerful, wise, and loving Lord, who is ready, willing, and able to handle anything we face. Nothing is impossible for Him (Luke 1:37).

Understanding this is central to overcoming our ingrained apprehensions, which is why these two principles will shape the remainder of our study of anxiety.

1. Fear Achieves Nothing of Value

For the remainder of this chapter, we will look at what being afraid does produce for us—the negative consequences that ongoing worry can have on our lives. This will help us determine once and for all whether the concerns we harbor or the negative emotions we face are due to deep, fearful wounds within us.

You see, there are times when we don't realize we are operating out of deep-seated worry and may even think we don't have a problem with fear. But those who've studied anxiety have concluded that it is universal—experienced by people of every culture and age group, during every era of history. No one is immune from it, no matter how hard we fight against it or how many defenses we attempt to construct.

Of course, there are people who adamantly deny ever feeling frightened, but in my experience they are some of the most fearful people of all. They build up their possessions, physique, influence, impressive qualifications, or what have you—all to prove they have nothing that could scare them. But in reality, they are terrified of losing the things that form the basis of their security. If their defenses collapse, they are absolutely devastated.

This brings us to the next principle—the foundation that never fails.

2. Trust in God Diminishes Fear

Our focus should be on our Father, who faithfully provides. As I often say, trusting God means looking beyond what we can see to what He sees. When our attention is trained on the challenges before us, they appear much more ominous and terrifying than they really are. But when we consider the immeasurable grandeur, strength, and brilliance of our awesome Creator—who formed the entire universe out of nothing just by speaking—our concerns really don't look so bad.

Sadly, there are issues that cloud our vision and understanding of the Father's love, power, and wisdom that keep us from fully trusting Him. They are wounds we may not even realize still have an effect on us but that create a continual breach in our relationship with Him. These subconscious fears become active roadblocks to our faith. We want to trust and obey God, but we cannot pinpoint why we're having so much trouble or how to overcome it.

> *Our subconscious fears become active roadblocks to our faith.*

For example, I experienced a time when I faced a terrible impediment to my faith. I couldn't understand why I was struggling so badly or why I was so agitated—everything else in my life seemed to be going very well. I recall repeatedly praying that the Lord would enable me to trust Him more. But for whatever reason, I just could not break through the impassable wall that kept me from relying on Him fully.

Finally, I asked my four closest friends for help. They were all wise men who loved God, so I knew they would give me excellent counsel. They committed themselves to staying with me—praying, asking questions, and discussing the events of my life—until the Father showed us what was really going on.

We met together and talked for about eight hours the first day and several more hours the following day. I recounted everything about my personal history I could recall. Finally I said, "That's everything I know to tell you. I don't think I held anything back."

One of the men nodded and suggested, "Charles, put your head on the table and close your eyes." I did so. He then asked me a question I will never forget.

"Imagine that your father just picked you up in his arms and held you. What do you feel?" He went straight to the core of my problem and I burst into tears. I could not stop weeping for quite a while.

You see, my father passed away when I was only nine months old. Losing him at that young age created profound areas of emptiness and uncertainty within me I didn't even realize were there.

When I settled down, my friend again asked, "What do you feel, Charles?"

"I feel warm, secure, and accepted. I feel loved," I replied. For the first time I truly understood that God loved me—that I could have a real, personal relationship with Him beyond salvation. Please realize, I had been preaching about the Lord's unconditional love all of my life. I believed it with my mind, but had never experienced it deep within my spirit until that day.

Had I ever told myself that the Lord didn't really love me? No. Did I ever doubt God's love? No. So what was it within me that created that inability to experience the Father's love in a meaningful way?

It was the need a little boy had for his earthly father that was never met. My mind learned to block out the pain, do without his physical presence, and survive. No one was at fault. My mother loved me very much and did the best she could. She was a wonderful mother. But I needed my father, and that affected how my mind processed information about the Lord. The most amazing thing of all was that I had absolutely no idea those self-protective thought patterns even existed until they were exposed.

Imagining God holding me as an earthly dad holds his little boy was just what I needed in order to overcome that roadblock. I affectionately carried my son Andy that way many times, but had never even considered how much I needed to be held by my own father—and especially my heavenly Father.

Suddenly, my struggle with God made sense, and I finally felt close to Him. Recognizing His presence in such an intensely tangible way opened the floodgates of profound relief and joy. It was groundbreaking. Coming to that understanding—having that hidden wound revealed and healed—changed my entire life and ministry.

Friend, you don't know what you don't know about yourself. None of us do. Uncovering the hidden wounds requires the work of the Holy Spirit, who is able to examine and minister to us in extraordinary ways (Rom. 8:26–27). He may use Scripture, godly counsel, circumstances, sermons, or other resources—but without the Spirit of the living God revealing those secret places of pain in you, they will remain concealed (1 Cor. 2:11–14).

> *You don't know what you don't know about yourself.*

So when we move on to the next chapter and we look at what issues may be getting in the way of you fully trusting the Father, I hope you will consider each prayerfully and be open to what He has to say to you.

THE TELLTALE SIGNS

For now, however, I ask you to focus on the symptoms of deeply ingrained anxiety. This is just as important as thinking through the causes because this is the first step in determining if you have some blind spots in your emotional life. So please consider each of these consequences carefully. And as you discover the signs of anxiety in your life, write them down so you can bring each to the Father in prayer.

1. A Persistent Lack of Peace

The first and most obvious result of deep-seated fear, of course, is a lack of peace. We feel as if something is off, amiss, or out of control. The New Testament word for *anxiety* sheds some light on this. It is used in 1 Peter 5:6–7, "Humble yourselves under the mighty hand of God . . . casting all your *anxiety* on Him, because He cares for you" (emphasis added). The Greek term used there is *merimna*, which comes from a root that means "pulled apart," "split into pieces," or "disjointed." In other words, there is something within that is always tugging us in a different direction, diverting our attention, and preventing us from focusing on the task before us. It gnaws at us continually, making us feel uneasy, dissatisfied, and distracted.

This dividing force within us stands in direct opposition to the concept of *peace*, which is *eirene* in the Greek. Jesus used it when He said, "These things I have spoken to you, so that in Me you may have *peace*" (John 16:33, emphasis added). It is a word that means "joined or bound together." For example, through Jesus' sacrifice on the cross we can have *peace*—or *be united*—with Him and be fully reconciled to the Father (Col. 1:20).

However, it also means an internal sense of harmony and tranquillity. Everything within us is calm—confident "that God causes all things to work together for good to those who love God, to those who are called according to His purpose" (Rom. 8:28). It is the Savior's goal that we would possess the inward composure that comes from having a personal relationship with Him and enjoying His provision. How do I know this? Because of what He said in John 14:27, "Peace I leave with you; My peace I give to you; not as the world gives do I give to you. Do not let your heart be troubled, nor let it be fearful."

He doesn't want you to be torn apart from the inside. Rather, His desire is that you have the quiet stillness of trusting Him as your Lord.

So ask yourself if there is anything that is tearing you apart. Do you have tranquillity in your innermost soul or do you feel a constant agitation? If you are unsure, pray for God to reveal anything that is persistently stealing your serenity. Then thank Him for rooting out those concerns that are pulling you apart and teaching you His peace.

2. A Divided Mind

As you can imagine, if your inner person is disjointed, it is likely that your mind will be pulled in different directions as well. Therefore, if you have ingrained fear, you may find it difficult to concentrate on the tasks or duties at hand.

There are several ways this can reveal itself in your life and how you deal with the choices you face. So as you go forward through each indication that fear is ruling the mind, please ask yourself, *Is this evident in me?*

First, because anxiety is a constant and wearying distraction, it often prevents us from focusing on our assignments—from completing them as quickly, effectively, and as skillfully as we are capable of. Our productivity, energy levels, and performance are impacted.

For example, many experience this to a heightened degree when loved ones are in the hospital or receiving intensive care. They are so consumed with worry, they find themselves emotionally spent, unable to fully concentrate on the task before them, and merely going through the motions of completing their duties. When a loved one is in a critical condition, this is understandable.

However, what I am referring to is a much more subtle but persistent inability to focus. When we are distracted on an ongoing basis, we will not be able to give our best, improve in our abilities, and learn important new skill sets or accomplish the objectives that are dear to our hearts. Ultimately, this lack of concentration will have implications for our income, success at work, and achievement of goals.

Second, we may struggle with indecision. When we struggle with deep woundedness, it is sometimes difficult for us to step forward in confidence because we are so afraid of taking a wrong turn or missing something better. Seeing too many options often increases our unease and makes our decisions much more challenging.

For instance, many young people who come from broken homes experience intense uncertainty when choosing a mate. They don't want to repeat the mistakes their parents made, so they either refuse to seek a mate at all or they continue their dating relationships for years without ever making a commitment. Rather than seeking God's will and trusting Him to lead them in the right way at the right time, they abstain from the decision and end up missing a great blessing the Father has for them.

Although this is a relational example, the problem of indecision can permeate every area of our lives—paralyzing us from letting go of the things that hinder us and taking hold of all that the Lord has planned for us. If you are having difficulty stepping out in faith, this underlying trepidation may have something to do with it.

Third, our apprehensions can drive us to make unwise decisions. Although fear immobilizes some people, it can have the opposite effect on us as well—compelling us to jump at opportunities because we are afraid of missing out.

A good example of the rash actions we take when we are motivated by fear can be seen clearly in the biblical account of 1 Samuel 13. Saul's impertinent rush to secure God's favor resulted in terrible consequences that would haunt him for the rest of his life.

Verse 5 tells us, "The Philistines assembled to fight with Israel, 30,000 chariots and 6,000 horsemen, and people like the sand which is on the seashore in abundance." The Israelites were so terrified by the threat of this great foreign army that they "hid themselves in caves, in thickets, in cliffs, in cellars, and in pits. Also some of the Hebrews crossed the Jordan into the land of Gad and Gilead" (vv. 6–7).

King Saul understood that for Israel to be victorious in the battle against the Philistines, God would have to help them supernaturally. After all, he had only "about six hundred men" (v. 15) to stand with him against the enormous Philistine army. There was no way the Israelites could hold off such a powerful enemy without the Lord's intervention.

The problem was that as king, Saul had no right to make the sacrifices that God had commanded. That privilege and responsibility went to the prophet Samuel, who had instructed, "Behold, I will come down to you to offer burnt offerings and sacrifice peace offerings. You shall wait seven days until I come to you and show you what you should do" (1 Sam. 10:8). However, as the seventh day drew to a close, Saul grew increasingly anxious and impatient because Samuel was nowhere to be found. The Philistines were posed for war, and the people were beginning to desert him.

Driven by fear, Saul jumped. He ran ahead of God's plan and made the sacrifices himself. Sadly, Scripture reveals that "As soon as he finished offering the burnt offering, behold, Samuel came" (13:10). If he had only waited just a little longer, the Lord would have blessed him greatly. But the anxiety within him drove him to ruin.

As a result, Samuel proclaimed, "You have acted foolishly; you have not kept the commandment of the LORD your God, which He commanded you, for now *the* LORD *would have established your kingdom over Israel forever. But now your kingdom shall not endure*" (13:13–14, emphasis added).

Ultimately, Saul lost the kingdom because his panic drove him to make an unwise decision. We do likewise when we allow our fears to influence our choices such as taking a job, selecting a spouse, making a large purchase, or what have you.

Therefore, if you ever find yourself driven by the thought, *If I don't act now, I'll miss the opportunity and may never have another chance*—rather than whether or not that choice is God's will for you—then it is likely that you're acting out of anxiety and you will not come to a wise conclusion. My advice to you is, "Wait for the LORD; be strong and let your heart take courage; yes, wait for the LORD" (Ps. 27:14). Allow Him to tell you "yes," "no," or "wait" in the matter. Then when He shows you what to do, you can step out confidently in faith. Certainly, the Father will never steer you wrong and will bless your obedience.

> *When you act out*
> *of anxiety,*
> *you will not come*
> *to a wise conclusion.*

3. Diminished Self-Confidence

For this next symptom of deep-seated anxiety, let me ask you: Do you measure up? Do you have what it takes to be successful or to be loved and respected by others? Do you feel good about yourself?

Or are you constantly second-guessing yourself—perpetually concerned that you'll be rejected, deemed unworthy, or found to be inadequate? Are there parts of you—your personality, looks, abilities, or attributes—that you just cannot stand? Do you ever feel helpless to change those aspects of your life? Do you wonder if you'll ever be good enough to deserve the desires of your heart?

If any of those questions strike a chord within you, it may be an indication that you are struggling with insecurity and that fear has prevented you from understanding who God created you to be.

These anxieties can be so embedded in the way we think that they seem to be an immovable part of our personhood—we truly believe this is who we are and who we'll always be. We worry that we will never do anything right, that we will not belong, and that we will be found unworthy of love and respect.

Consequently, we may isolate ourselves from others, work hard to make people like us, and fail to step out in faith when the Lord calls. We may even verbalize doubts about our abilities or put ourselves down when we talk so that others won't expect too much of us. However, all of these symptoms prove that fear has damaged our self-confidence and is dominating our lives.

These are some of the most difficult misgivings for people to overcome because they are part of our identity, which is powerfully affixed within us. In order to heal, we must confront and accept the very flaws and failures we try so hard to hide from everyone else (2 Cor. 12:7–10). We must also change what we define as valuable about ourselves. Instead of dwelling on whether or not we will fail,

> *We must intentionally focus on the fact that God loves us and is always faithful to us.*

if people will dislike us, or if we'll get what we want, we must intentionally focus on the fact that God loves us and is always faithful to us (Phil. 3:4–14).

Of course, overcoming this mind-set is far easier said than done. As I said, those anxieties are particularly difficult to root out. I've even heard people try to spiritualize their entrenched doubts about themselves by saying they are just being humble. However, true biblical humility does not require that you disparage yourself, and it would never call into question how God created you (Ps. 139:14). This does not honor Him in the least.

Nineteenth-century pastor Dr. J. R. Miller tells us, "What is humility? It is not thinking meanly of one's self. It is not a voluntary humbling of one's self for any particular purpose. It is the spirit which is ready always to use its best powers and its richest gifts in the lowliest service of love. Love is at the heart of it. . . . Humility is in the spirit, not in the station."

In other words, if we have humble hearts, we will be willing to do whatever God calls us to do out of love for our Savior. It does not mean we despise ourselves. On the contrary, it often takes a person whose self-confidence is firmly rooted in Christ to do the difficult tasks He assigns (Acts 5:40–42). But if you continually dread failure, doubt that you will be accepted, or question whether or not you measure up, then there may be a festering wound of fear within you.

4. Damaged Relationships

You and I were created to be in relationship with God and others. But when we are plagued with doubt—when we lack peace, have low self-confidence, or struggle with a divided mind—our woundedness affects our interactions with those around us. As you read through these consequences, however, please understand, there are many ways that our anxieties can affect our relationships. I am simply highlighting four of the most extreme so you can have an idea of what to look for in your own life.

First, due to fears, we may unconsciously protect ourselves because we are suspicious of others' intentions or feel we don't measure up.

When we mistrust people as a general rule, we tend to make sure that no one gets too close to us by hiding our real thoughts and sentiments. We isolate ourselves, doing whatever we can to make sure no one hurts us.

Unfortunately, this usually results in feelings of alienation and loneliness because we do not get our deepest emotional needs met.

So if you feel isolated or estranged from those you want to be close to, ask yourself, *Do I push people away when I sense they are getting too attached or personal? Am I inordinately guarded with others?* If so, it may be because you subconsciously prevent yourself from being vulnerable to others due to ingrained fear. Thankfully, God can show you who to trust and how to exercise wisdom and discretion in your relationships.

Second, we may wish to connect with others but become so inwardly focused that we have trouble reaching out to them. In order to have relationships with other people, it is necessary for us to show interest in them—listening to their feelings, dreams, hopes, and desires. We must engage with them, find areas of commonality, and be willing to support them when they experience times of difficulty.

Unfortunately, we can become so accustomed to focusing on our own issues that we find it challenging to care for others. We may feel awkward when reaching out or may dread being rejected if we do so.

However, if we refuse to take the risk, we will never have the meaningful relationships that Christ intended us to have. We will turn people off with our self-focus and uneasiness because they will interpret our standoffishness as arrogance, rather than a cry for friendship.

Third, we may wish to bond with others to fulfill our own needs but be so inwardly focused that we have no interest in giving back to them. This is very similar to the previous issue, but it applies to the person who has developed the social skills to keep others providing for them despite their lack of engagement.

These individuals take as much as they can but give back as little as possible. Their sense of self-protection is so overdeveloped that they never realize the joy of sharing generously with others or that "it is more blessed to give than to receive" (Acts 20:35). Sadly, we see more of this every day. Yet we should not be surprised that this type of behavior has its roots in fear as well.

I've read about several children who were so neglected in their early infancy—abandoned for hours and days at a time—that they became emotionally shut off and unable to care about others without serious intervention. I can only imagine the profound terror those babies felt as they cried out and no one paid attention to them. It is no wonder their hearts hardened in self-protection. But I am convinced even this kind of overwhelming, isolating fear can be healed through God's loving power.

Fourth, we can become so needy because of our anxieties that we exhaust those we love. When we require our friends and family members to give us constant assurance of their agreement, care, or acceptance, it can become quite burdensome to them.

Perhaps there is someone you dread seeing because of the way he or she drains your energy. It may be that the individual grumbles nonstop about the same burdens, worries, and grievances year after year. Or it could be that he is constantly looking to you for validation and you just don't know what else to say to him.

Ultimately, these individuals refuse to heed any advice, make progress, or relinquish their complaints because voicing their concerns is the way they get attention. The result is that those who have the misfortune of encountering them are left feeling depleted, anxious, and frustrated.

We know how trying this type of personality can be, so it is a good idea to ask our loved ones if we demand too much of them or if our own need for approval has become overwhelming.

5. Poor Health

Of course, one of the most intriguing ways that fear is demonstrated in our lives is in the way it shows up in our bodies. I've known many people who appeared content on the outside, but whose internalized apprehensions resulted in high blood pressure, heart and respiratory problems, and digestive distress. In fact, numerous medical and scientific studies have concluded that anxiety is related to these and many other health-related conditions, such as asthma, colitis, ulcers, muscle weakness, autoimmune diseases, vertigo, psoriasis, eczema, headaches, and even cancer. Why is this?

It all has to do with the way our mind and emotions affect our bodies. God built us with everything we need in order to react to sudden emergencies through what is called the *fight-or-flight response.* As we saw earlier in this chapter, if we receive news that requires us to leap to attention, are attacked in some way, or encounter danger—such as coming across a mountain lion or rattlesnake on a hike—our bodies instantly trigger their defenses. Our heartbeat and respiratory rate quicken; our cortisol and adrenaline levels increase; the blood and nutrient flow to our muscle groups and limbs are augmented; our nervous system is mobilized; and our pupils dilate. Everything we need to preserve ourselves is primed for action. The processes that are not immediately needed for survival—such as our digestive and immune systems—are inhibited, allowing more energy to go to essential areas. A great deal happens to make our bodies as effective as possible in fighting or fleeing.

We can see the awesome wisdom the Lord had in giving us this capability. However, the Father meant for this to be a short-term provision for emergencies. He did not design us to live in a perpetual state of extreme stress, which is what we often do. Imagine the harm we do ourselves when these biological systems stay in this heightened condition. It is no wonder that when we consciously or subconsciously harbor anxiety, there is a notable effect on our health.

6. An Impediment to Spiritual Growth

The final and potentially most devastating effect of persistent anxiety in our lives is that it hinders us from becoming all that the Father created us to be. How does fear keep us floundering in our relationship with the Lord?

First, our anxiety deters us from trusting the Father and being conformed to His character. We know that one of the main ways the Lord instructs us, frees us from bondage, and forms His likeness in us is through difficulties. I often say, because it is true, adversity is a bridge to a deeper relationship with God because it is true. If our hearts are inclined toward Him, the tests we experience can fortify our faith (1 Pet. 1:6–7), strengthen our endurance (James 1:2–4), prove our character (Rom. 5:3–5), and give us a platform for ministry (2 Cor. 1:3–7).

However, fear generally causes us to be pessimistic, self-focused, and unwilling to take risks. We ask, *Why me?* instead of, *Father, what is it You are teaching me?* If we are suspicious of His intentions or believe that He is constantly sending us trials without purpose or meaning, it will be impossible for us to trust Him fully or draw nearer to Him, which is ultimately what He calls us to do (Prov. 3:5–6). Because of this, we will fail to learn what He is teaching us.

So ask yourself, *What do I really believe when I face difficulties? Do I question God's character? Do I wonder if He despises me? Do I feel like He is punishing me without cause? Or do I give Him thanks because I know He has promised to work all things together for my good* (Rom. 8:28)?

In other words, do you express your confidence in Him? Or do you allow your apprehensions to taint your view of what He is accomplishing?

The apostle John explains, "We have come to know and have believed the love which God has for us. God is love, and the one who abides in love abides in God, and God abides in him. . . . There is no fear in love; but perfect love casts out fear, because fear involves punishment, and the one who fears is not perfected in love" (1 John 4:16, 18). The Father cares for you deeply and unconditionally. He allows certain challenges in your life so He can teach you to walk more closely with Him. You can be confident that "He disciplines us for our good, so that we may share His holiness" (Heb. 12:10).

> *The Father cares for you deeply and unconditionally. He allows certain challenges in your life so He can teach you to walk more closely with Him.*

But if you doubt that God really loves you and you're continually terrified about where and how He will send the next trial, then there is something terribly wrong with how you view Him. Your understanding of Him is not only distorted but it is also dangerous because it is keeping you from relating intimately with the One who cares for you most. This brings us to our next point.

Second, our anxieties hinder us from hearing the Father and responding to Him in obedience. Hebrews 11:6 instructs, "Without faith it is impossible to please Him, for he who comes to God must believe that He is and that He is a rewarder of those who seek Him." In other words, complete trust should characterize the life of His children.

We know that the great men and women of God were commended for their absolute reliance upon the Lord and confidence in His unfailing character. Against unbelievable odds and staggering adversaries they "conquered kingdoms, performed acts of righteousness, obtained promises, shut the mouths of lions, quenched the power of fire, escaped the edge of the sword, from weakness were made strong, became mighty in war, put foreign armies to flight" (Heb. 11:33–34) all because they trusted the Father and wanted to honor Him. They did not focus on the things that could go wrong or the magnitude of the challenges; rather, they "endured, as seeing Him who is unseen" (Heb. 11:27). And the Lord rewarded their devotion by giving them awesome victories.

But if we are full of anxiety, we may cringe at the prospect of joining their ranks. We can be terrified that God would make us experience such hardship and sacrifice. As a result, we shy away from the opportunities that would grow our faith or strengthen our relationship with Him. We don't pray because of what He might say. We don't even claim His promises because we doubt they could be meant for us.

In doing so, we may believe we are keeping ourselves safe. But don't be fooled—we are hurting ourselves immeasurably because we are missing out on God's best for our lives. As we saw in the account of Adam and Eve in the previous chapter, the enemy's favorite tools for hindering us are fear and uncertainty. He puts devastating, faithless doubts in our minds: *Am I sure I heard God right? Who really receives direction from Him anyway? Am I certain He will really help me? After all, He doesn't really have time to help someone as insignificant as me. I'm worthless. Look at my misery—He's probably upset with me. He can't use me; I'm too weak. I certainly don't deserve His favor. And look around—everything is against me. There is no evidence He is helping me, so forget Him. Better to quit while I'm ahead than be humiliated.*

Do these thoughts enter your mind when you try to obey the Father? Do they keep you from stepping out in faith? The enemy knows just how to chip away at your convictions of the Lord's love and provision and keep you from becoming an effective believer. For Adam and Eve, that meant the fall of the human race, a lifetime of hardship, and the loss of their intimate communion with God. For you and me, it means we will forfeit the abundant life—the one that is worth living and that would truly satisfy our souls.

This is why we must make a conscious effort to choose God over our apprehensions and to replace the enemy's disheartening messages with the Word of God.

> *Make a conscious effort to choose God over your apprehensions and to replace the enemy's disheartening messages with the Word of God.*

Think about it. Courage is not the lack of fear, but the determination that there is One who is greater than anything that could come against us. You can be brave and courageous. God can use you in mighty ways you've never even imagined—filling you with a love, joy, and peace you never dreamed possible. But you must accept that what He says is absolutely true: "The LORD is the one who goes ahead of you; He will be with you. He will not fail you or forsake you. Do not fear or be dismayed" (Deut. 31:8). And whenever the devastating lies of the enemy come into your mind, you must counteract them with God's truth.

THE ENEMY'S LIE	GOD'S TRUTH— OUR DEFENSE
Am I sure I heard God right?	Trust in the LORD with all your heart and do not lean on your own understanding. In all your ways acknowledge Him, and He will make your paths straight. —PROVERBS 3:5–6
Who really receives direction from Him anyway?	I will instruct you and teach you in the way which you should go; I will counsel you with My eye upon you. —PSALM 32:8
Am I certain He will really help me?	Ask, and it will be given to you; seek, and you will find; knock, and it will be opened to you. For everyone who asks receives, and he who seeks finds, and to him who knocks it will be opened. —MATTHEW 7:7–8

THE ENEMY'S LIE	GOD'S TRUTH— OUR DEFENSE
He doesn't really have time to help someone as insignificant as me.	Thus says the LORD, your Creator, O Jacob, and He who formed you, O Israel, "Do not fear, for I have redeemed you; I have called you by name; you are Mine! When you pass through the waters, I will be with you." —ISAIAH 43:1–2
I'm worthless.	See how great a love the Father has bestowed on us, that we would be called children of God. —1 JOHN 3:1
Look at my misery— He's probably upset with me.	The LORD is near to the brokenhearted and saves those who are crushed in spirit. —PSALM 34:18

THE ENEMY'S LIE	GOD'S TRUTH— OUR DEFENSE
He can't use me— I'm too weak.	My grace is sufficient for you, for My power is perfected in weakness. —2 CORINTHIANS 12:9
I certainly don't deserve His favor.	The LORD longs to be gracious to you, and therefore He waits on high to have compassion on you. For the LORD is a God of justice; how blessed are all those who long for Him. —ISAIAH 30:18
Look around— everything is against me.	"No weapon that is formed against you will prosper; and every tongue that accuses you in judgment you will condemn. This is the heritage of the servants of the LORD, and their vindication is from Me," declares the LORD. —ISAIAH 54:17

THE ENEMY'S LIE	GOD'S TRUTH— OUR DEFENSE
There is no evidence He is helping me, so forget Him.	For momentary, light affliction is producing for us an eternal weight of glory far beyond all comparison, while we look not at the things which are seen, but at the things which are not seen; for the things which are seen are temporal, but the things which are not seen are eternal. —2 CORINTHIANS 4:17–18
Better to quit while I'm ahead than be humiliated.	The Lord GOD helps Me, therefore, I am not disgraced; therefore, I have set My face like flint, and I know that I will not be ashamed. —ISAIAH 50:7

FREEDOM THROUGH CHANGE

Do you experience any of the symptoms of anxiety? Does a persistent lack of peace plague you? Are you tormented by a divided mind—your life characterized by a lack of focus, progress, and wisdom in making decisions? Do you constantly second-guess yourself because of the fear that you'll be rejected, deemed unworthy, or found to be inadequate? Are your relationships strained, unfulfilling, and, at times, even alienating? Is your body deteriorating as a result of undue stress? Have you found yourself unable to grow spiritually as you hoped you would?

If you answered yes to any or all of these, then there is evidence that some form of anxiety is driving you. Friend, I say this with all sincerity, you need to deal with your fears in God's strength and wisdom in order to enjoy the freedom He created you to experience.

You need to deal with your fears in God's strength and wisdom in order to enjoy the freedom He created you to experience.

I realize this may be intimidating for you. It is for most of us. I recall teaching about liberty from fear one Sunday morning some years ago. After the service, a woman came up to speak with me about the message because she wasn't convinced she could truly let go of her anxieties. After a few minutes, the real source of her disbelief was revealed.

"But how will I feel? I mean, what will I think about if I let my worries go?" she asked with tears in her eyes.

I was taken off guard, but only for a moment. Sometimes we

grow so accustomed to our anxieties that they become part of our identity and a refuge for us. We realize that if we let them go, we may encounter situations that will challenge us—making us feel awkward and uncomfortable. For example, the person with a fear of flying may use his trepidation as an excuse to avoid traveling altogether. He may say, "I would love to go overseas on a mission trip, but I am so afraid of airplanes, I couldn't possibly go." He uses his phobia of flying as a justification to avoid what God may be genuinely calling him to do—a task that will test him, push him outside his comfort zone, and require him to exhibit faith.

Likewise, you may be holding on to some of your fears because they've become a crutch—an excuse for other failings in your life. But as long as you cling to them, you're missing out on God's best for your life.

So before you move on to the next chapter and learn about the issues that may be getting in the way of you fully trusting the Father, commit yourself to letting go of your fears. I want to assure you, there is awesome freedom and joy in releasing them to Him. Yes, it may be intimidating and unnerving at first, but it is absolutely worth it.

Therefore, be open to what the Lord has to say to you, confront your fears with faith, and obey the Father with confidence of His awesome plans for your life. His wonderful blessings await you. Don't miss out on them any longer.

||||||||||||||||||||||||||||||||||||||||||||||||||||||||||||||||||||||||||||||||||||||||||||||||||||||||||

Father, how grateful I am that You have begun to reveal all the ways that fear is ingrained in my life. Thank You for releasing me from the bondage it causes. I agree with You that my anxieties do not achieve anything of value and that my focus should be on You—my faithful, loving Savior, who always provides perfectly.

Therefore, Father, I ask You to root out these places of woundedness and pain. You alone know where I lack peace and confidence—where the concerns of life tear me apart—so I commit them to Your tender care. Wherever I am tormented by a divided mind or hide myself for fear of being rejected, deemed unworthy, or found to be inadequate, please heal me. Unearth the coping mechanisms that cause me to be isolated from my loved ones and destructive in my relationships. Mend my body from all the ways it has been broken by stress and worry. Teach me how to enjoy the quiet stillness of trusting You as my unfailing and loving Lord. Destroy the doubts that have become roadblocks to my faith. And empower me to reject the enemy's lies and replace them with truth from Your Word.

Father, I confess that some of my fears have become a crutch—I've grown comfortable with them and use them as an excuse to avoid stepping out in faith. But Lord, I don't want to live this way anymore. I recognize that my anxieties are keeping me in bondage and preventing me from experiencing Your very best for my life.

Therefore, Lord God, I commit myself to You, with full confidence that You lead me on the path of freedom and joy. Thank You for giving me the peace that passes understanding. In Jesus' name I pray. Amen.

QUESTIONS FOR
PERSONAL REFLECTION AND GROUP STUDY

1. Think about the issues you usually worry about. Are most of your concerns valid or are they merely perceived problems?

2. Is there any problem you tend to think about incessantly? Why do you think this particular trial is such an issue for you?

3. Can you think of a situation in which you struggled with indecision to the point of missing a blessing from God? What kept you from making a commitment?

4. Have you ever rushed ahead of God out of anxiety? What was the result?

5. In reading through this chapter, did you discover any of the telltale signs of anxiety in your own life? What were they?

6. If you recognized the consequences of deep-seated

fear in yourself, consider how you have protected yourself in those areas. What steps could you take to turn them over to God?

7. Name a source of anxiety on your mind today. Take time to research what the Bible teaches about that issue (if that particular problem is not addressed in Scripture, think about general biblical principles that would apply to your situation). Are you willing to commit that situation to the Lord, with faith that He will take care of it?

5

THE COURAGE TO STAND

Conquering Fear Through a Change of Focus

I HAVE GOT TO GET OFF this plane—right NOW!

That, of course, was impossible. The pilot had announced we were cruising at an altitude of more than 35,000 feet. There was no getting off—at least, not for a while.

But it didn't matter. My body was in full crisis mode. My thoughts raced. My heart pounded. I couldn't catch my breath. Everything inside me shook with fear.

I looked at the emergency exit and began to contemplate my options. *I wonder if I can get that door open. I need to get air. I HAVE TO GET OUT!*

I knew I was thinking irrationally, but I couldn't stop myself. It was a commercial airliner, so I pushed the button for the flight attendant. When she arrived, I told her about the all-consuming and powerful anxiety that had suddenly enveloped me. She found a doctor on board who then sat with me and asked me what was wrong.

I told him I was experiencing an overwhelming feeling of

being trapped and that I needed to get off the plane. He said, "Well, you know you can't."

I responded, "Yes sir, I know I can't. But the desire is absolutely overpowering." He probed a little further, asking me questions about my life—my occupation, why I was on the flight, and so forth. As we talked, I admitted to him that I was going through a very trying time. I was struggling with news that was extremely difficult to accept—and was even more impossible to deal with effectively. As we talked it through, he encouraged me and the panic began to subside.

It has been more than twenty years since that experience, but it taught me something very important: *For us to overcome our fears, it is crucial we unearth where they originate from, which then shows us what thoughts trigger them.*

> *For us to overcome our fears, it is crucial we unearth where they originate from, which then shows us what thoughts trigger them.*

That doctor was very wise for investigating the initiating source of my anxiety rather than just dismissing me as a nervous traveler. After all, it wasn't the flying that actually terrified me. I had been fine for the first hour and a half of the flight, so that couldn't be the true cause of my fear. Rather, as I contemplated the impossible situation I was facing, I recognized there was nothing I could do about it, and I was afraid of the consequences. As this awareness grew, so did the discomfort of occasional turbulence, the annoyance at the level of noise in the aircraft's cabin, and the sense of being trapped and completely out of control.

Eventually, as my uneasiness escalated, I wrongly attributed my anxiety to the plane ride itself, rather than to the real cause of my distress. I was only able to calm down once the doctor identified the difficult circumstances I was facing as triggering my emotions. I was then able to give the situation to God fully and counteract my apprehensions with truth from His Word.

ORIGINATING SOURCES

This is true for you as well. It is exceedingly important to find the origins of your fears so that you can then deal with them—and the thoughts they generate in you—effectively. Otherwise, you are only addressing the surface symptoms of your anxiety, rather than the profound issues that make you feel helpless and out of control.

For example, one area of intense anxiety that I struggled with throughout most of my ministry was that I wouldn't be prepared to preach on Sunday morning. Especially in my early years as a pastor, I worried that I would not be able to deliver the message or that I would somehow let the Father and the congregation down. I'd constantly wake up in the middle of the night thinking, "God, suppose I'm not ready? What will I do?" This apprehension caused me to spend long hours studying Scripture, praying fervently, committing myself to the Lord, and depending upon Him. But all that effort didn't matter. I would still fret about the sermon right up until the moment I reached the pulpit.

I didn't have freedom from this fear until I pinpointed the true reason it bothered me. I asked myself, *Why am I so afraid of not being ready? God loves me. The church supports me. I've been called to preach. Why am I so fearful of delivering the message?* I thought it was because I wanted to see the Lord's awesome work in people's lives so badly—which I truly did. But that wasn't the reason I was troubled. I acknowledged that any transformation in people's lives was the work of the Holy Spirit.

So after a great deal of introspection, I realized that what I was really frightened of was looking like a failure and being criticized—which is connected to other events in my life. Thankfully, when I took that concern to the Father and sought His guidance in dealing with it, I found freedom. I am happy to say I don't wrestle with that fear anymore.

> *When I took that concern to the Father and sought His guidance in dealing with it, I found freedom.*

I want you to find liberty from your apprehensions as well. So with this in mind, let us look at some of the common sources of anxiety. As we go through them, please think about the fears you struggle with and consider where they may come from.

1. Attitudes We're Taught as Children

It is absolutely amazing how much you and I learn as young children. From the time we are born, we interact with our surroundings, observe the members of our families, and are taught about the world by our parents or caregivers. Unfortunately, this often means we are trained early in life—at times deliberately, but more often unintentionally, through their comments and reactions—to fear the things that they do. These anxieties become ingrained deep within us, because once we hear them expressed and feel their impact, they become part of how we relate to the world around us.

I can still remember how my mother used to say, "Don't get close to the river, Charles. You might fall in and drown." She was speaking out of her love for me, of course, but my young mind naturally concluded that water was inherently dangerous. It took quite a while before I could summon the courage to get into the creek and learn how to swim.

Likewise, when you learn a principle early in life from an authority figure whom you love and admire—such as a parent, family member, pastor, or teacher—you never fully forget it. It takes a great deal of intentional effort to overcome what is modeled to you and to replace it with God's truth and perspective.

It takes a great deal of intentional effort to overcome what is modeled to you and to replace it with God's truth and perspective.

For example, I once knew a man who did his very best to appear brave, unemotional, and invulnerable. But when great adversity arose in his life, he absolutely crumbled beneath the weight of the trial. Interestingly, it wasn't the actual problems that plagued him—it was that he could not handle the disquieting feelings of dread and panic that were rising up in him. I spoke to him for quite a while, trying to discern the true source of his concern.

"I don't think my father ever felt fear," he eventually told me. Because he never saw his father express his anxieties, the man assumed that any emotion was unmanly and undignified. The trouble he was facing was justifiably distressing, but he felt like a terrible failure because of his inability to overcome his feelings.

I replied, "I think your father probably felt a great deal of fear just like the rest of us. But he most likely refused to admit it because he was afraid of appearing weak—just as you are now. But remember that the strongest man who ever lived—our Savior, Jesus—experienced and showed very deep emotion. There is nothing wrong with that. If our holy, almighty God can express His feelings, you can too."

Likewise, there may be attitudes and principles that you learned at an early age that influence how you react to situations and what you tell yourself. One excellent exercise is to ask God to help you uncover all of the suppositions that shape how you live. As He exposes those mind-sets and beliefs to you, write them down and ask Him to show you how they line up with His Word. You may be surprised at what He reveals.

2. *Our Imaginations*

Your creative mind is an amazing and powerful gift from God. When used for positive purposes such as glorifying the Father and serving others, it can be extremely helpful. For example, out of the human imagination have come astounding technological breakthroughs that have allowed In Touch Ministries to broadcast the gospel all over the world, regardless of whether a person can read or has electricity.

Unfortunately, the same imagination can become a prison for

us if employed in a negative manner. People can be dominated by what I call *shadow fears*—they fret about problems that aren't real and don't occur. Sadly, because of these baseless worries, they end up missing God's best for their lives.

Is your imagination more negatively inclined than it needs to be?

For example, I've known people who were very bright and successful, but because they never went to college or graduate school, they always worried that others would think they were uneducated or unqualified. Often these individuals were uncommonly wise and perceptive about situations, but their fears still plagued them. And because they imagined themselves less worthy than those who had achieved a higher level of education, it affected their response to situations. Yet what does Scripture say? "Our adequacy is from God" (2 Cor. 3:5). It doesn't matter what your level of education is, who your family is, how much wealth or power you have—your significance comes from the Lord.

Throughout the years, I've also noticed that when some people lose friends or family members, they become fixated on the idea that other loved ones will be taken from them. These individuals become hyper-vigilant to any sign of sickness and agonize about normal, everyday activities such as driving in heavy traffic. Sadly, because of their preoccupation with death, they often miss out on opportunities to appreciate those close to them while they have them. The shadow fears completely consume them.

Does any of this sound like you? Are you wondering if your imagination is more negatively inclined than it needs to be? Perhaps you are not sure if you're struggling with shadow fears. If so, it is helpful to ask yourself the following questions:

- Do I ever say to myself, "God couldn't bless me because _____ ." Or, "They will not like me because _____."
- When facing a problem, do I usually worry that the worst will happen?
- Does imagining everything that could go wrong in a given situation ever prevent me from stepping out in faith?
- Are there issues that I fret about constantly—such as a loved one getting sick, people rejecting me, or losing everything I own—that actually have no basis in reality?

If so, then your imagination is most likely out of control and needs to be tamed. Ask God to redeem your creativity and help you "be transformed by the renewing of your mind, so that you may prove what the will of God is, that which is good and acceptable and perfect" (Rom. 12:2). And stop contemplating all the negative things that could happen to you and your loved ones. Rather, "whatever is true, whatever is honorable, whatever is right, whatever is pure, whatever is lovely, whatever is of good repute, if there is any excellence and if anything worthy of praise, dwell on these things . . . and the God of peace will be with you" (Phil. 4:8–9).

3. Lack of Information

The third possible source of our anxiety is a lack of information. The unknown can be terrifying. What we don't understand about our circumstances can cause us to be exceedingly fearful. What will the future hold? How will we overcome obstacles that are ahead? What if we cannot handle the troubles that we encounter?

These fears tend to fall into three categories:

1. Information that we recognize is incomplete
2. Information we may not realize is inadequate
3. Information that we cannot know

Most of us have experienced the apprehension that occurs when we recognize our information is incomplete. In fact, we probably felt it as early as grade school. As we took quizzes and tests, we wondered how difficult the questions would be and if they would be beyond our comprehension of the subject matter. The better we understood the topic, the more confidence we had going into the exams. But if we failed to study or if the material was very complex, we would naturally feel anxiety.

Another example is when we receive a diagnosis or report that we don't quite recognize and we realize we need to do some research. For instance, say you were feeling somewhat run-down, so you went to your local clinic. After an examination, the doctor informed you that you have *acute coryza* that is *afebrile*, and that there's no known cure. This news would most likely cause you some anxiety—unless you are a medical professional, that is. You see, *acute coryza* is merely the scientific name for the common cold. The fact that it is *afebrile* simply means that you don't have a fever.

Understanding the information you're given makes all the difference—and often a lack of comprehension is easily fixed by a little study. This is why Proverbs 25:2 tells us, "It is the glory of God to conceal a matter, but the glory of kings is to search out a matter."

> *What we don't understand about our circumstances can cause us to be exceedingly fearful.*

Then there is the anxiety that arises from not realizing we don't have all the information we need. For example, it is amazing how many letters I receive from people who worry that they or a loved one have committed the unpardonable sin that Jesus speaks of in Matthew 12:31–32: "Any sin and blasphemy shall be forgiven people, but blasphemy against the Spirit shall not be forgiven. Whoever speaks a word against the Son of Man, it shall be forgiven him; but whoever speaks against the Holy Spirit, it shall not be forgiven him, either in this age or in the age to come." They fear that they've irrevocably offended the Lord and have been disqualified from salvation because of some unspeakable act.

Thankfully, those who write in usually recognize that they lack understanding about what Scripture teaches concerning the unpardonable sin and are seeking the truth. But I often wonder, *How many people live with this anxiety daily without realizing that they don't have the full story?*

If you struggle with this apprehension, let me put your mind at ease. The *only* sin that will not be forgiven is outright rejection of Jesus Christ as Savior through continued unbelief. In John 3:17–18, Jesus explains, "God did not send the Son into the world to judge the world, but that the world might be saved through Him. He who believes in Him is not judged; *he who does not believe has been judged already*, because he has not believed in the name of the only begotten Son of God" (emphasis added).

In other words, when you accept Jesus as your personal Savior, He becomes the payment for *all* your sins—past, present, and future (Col. 2:13–14). But if you refuse to believe in Christ, then you must bear all the consequences of your sin on your own—and that means eternal separation from God (John 3:36; Rom. 6:23).

> *When you accept Jesus as your personal Savior, He becomes the payment for all your sins—past, present, and future.*

An excellent example of the Lord's awesome grace and forgiveness is the apostle Paul. Before knowing Jesus as his Savior, he was called Saul, and Scripture reports he "began ravaging the church, entering house after house, and dragging off men and women, he would put them in prison" (Acts 8:3). Acts 9:1–2 also attests, "Breathing threats and murder against the disciples of the Lord, [Saul] went to the high priest, and asked for letters from him to the synagogues at Damascus, so that if he found any belonging to the Way, both men and women, he might bring them bound to Jerusalem."

Saul was intent on destroying the early church—preventing the spread of the gospel and trying to squelch the work that the

Spirit was doing in people's hearts. Even Jesus questioned him outright, "Saul, Saul, why are you persecuting Me?" (Acts 9:4). If anyone had committed an unpardonable sin, it seemed Saul was a likely candidate. Yet, years later, Paul testified,

> I used to scoff at the name of Christ. I hunted down His people, harming them in every way I could. But God had mercy on me because I didn't know what I was doing, for I didn't know Christ at that time. Oh, how kind our Lord was, for He showed me how to trust Him and become full of the love of Christ Jesus. How true it is, and how I long that everyone should know it, that Christ Jesus came into the world to save sinners—and I was the greatest of them all. *But God had mercy on me so that Christ Jesus could use me as an example to show everyone how patient He is with even the worst sinners, so that others will realize that they, too, can have everlasting life.* (1 Tim. 1:13–16, TLB, emphasis added)

If you've asked God to forgive you on the basis of the shed blood of Jesus Christ on the cross at Calvary, there is absolutely no way you can commit the unpardonable sin. He has forgiven *all* your sins (Rom. 6:23; 1 John 1:9). You have no reason to be afraid. Paul certainly wasn't (2 Tim. 1:12).

But the real point of this illustration is that sometimes you may be fearful because you have an incomplete understanding of a subject or situation. This may be due to all manner of reasons: the instruction you've received, a lack of experience in a certain area, or even an important relationship that is missing from your life—such as with your mother or father. In fact, you may not even be able to pinpoint where your comprehension falls short or why it is creating such dread in your life. However, it is important to recognize that these worries do not disqualify you from being loved by God or signify that you are somehow less worthy than others. Rather, it is simply an indication that you must seek the Lord's insight—as we must all do.

Therefore, when you are anxious, it's crucial to ask, "Is it possible that a lack of information is at the source of my apprehensions? Are there aspects of a relationship with God or with others that I don't quite understand and that are causing me to be frightened?" You are promised, "If any of you lacks wisdom, let him ask of God, who gives to all generously and without reproach, and it will be given to him" (James 1:5). Seek the Father through prayer and His Word. He will certainly show you what you need to know—or set you on the right track to find it.

Finally, our anxieties may arise from information that we cannot know. We all have questions and hopes about the future, but if we're not careful, they can become issues that consume us. For instance, I often hear people worrying about what the economy will be like in five or ten years and whether their investments will pay off. I've also known freshmen and sophomores in college who expressed fear that there wouldn't be employment for them when they finished their graduate studies. Certainly finance and business experts can make educated projections, but no one truly knows where the economy or job market will be in the future—or what is in store for each particular individual and investment.

Likewise, I frequently encounter single adults who fret about whether or not they will ever wed, young marrieds who are apprehensive about bringing children into this troubled world, and couples who anxiously calculate if they will be able to retire in the next ten to fifteen years.

Only God knows what will happen in the future or what turns our paths will take. This is why James 4:13–15 admonishes, "Come now, you who say, 'Today or tomorrow we will go to such and such a city, and spend a year there and engage in business and make a profit.' Yet you do not know what your life will be like tomorrow. You are just a vapor that appears for a little while and then vanishes away. Instead, you ought to say, 'If the Lord wills, we will live and also do this or that.'"

> *Only God knows what will happen in the future or what turns our paths will take.*

Yes, we should make plans and be wise about saving. But ultimately, none of us knows what God has in store.

This is why I base my life on the compass of Proverbs 3:5–6: "Trust in the LORD with all your heart and do not lean on your own understanding. In all your ways acknowledge Him, and He will make your paths straight." You and I may not know what our futures hold, but our loving heavenly Father does. And there is no one who can lead us more tenderly, wisely, and effectively into tomorrow. Of course, this brings up our next point.

4. A Wrong View of God's Nature

It may be that a great source of anxiety for you is God Himself. As we saw in Chapter 3, often the deepest root of our apprehensions is the fear of being exposed and found lacking in His presence. Hopefully, as you've been reading and praying, the Father has been revealing areas where you don't quite trust Him or where your understanding of Him is lacking. Your faulty view of how He cares for or provides for you may also be causing you a great deal of anxiety.

I recall praying about this very issue when I was in seminary. I did not feel secure in my relationship with the Father, and it troubled me terribly. To a large extent this apprehension had to do with my view of salvation, though it took some time and a great deal of seeking the Lord in prayer and through the Word before I realized it.

You see, when as a twelve-year-old boy I walked down the aisle to accept Jesus as my Savior and Lord, I can still remember very clearly that the pastor told me, "Charles, you grow up and be a good boy and God will bless you. And one of these days when you die, you'll go to heaven." My pastor was a godly man, who certainly loved the Lord and always cared for me, so I took his words to heart. I wanted to be a good boy who pleased God. But from that moment on, I thought that it was my responsibility to maintain my relationship with the Savior by perfect behavior. I had already lost my earthly father; there was no way I wanted to lose my heavenly Father or be separated from Him by sin.

So I began my Christian life like many others do—trying to be good, reading the Bible, praying, and doing all I knew to please Him. But I never felt it was enough. In the evenings, I would kneel down by my bed and repent of whatever I could think of. After all, I believed that if I sinned, I was no longer saved—I no longer had a relationship with the Lord. I can remember begging, "Oh God, whatever I've done, I pray that You'll forgive me. Please, please forgive me, Father. Don't let me die without You." I went to sleep every night scared of what could happen to me.

But then one evening, I was praying as usual, and something within me—it had to be the Spirit of God—attested to the fact that what I believed *could not be true.* I didn't feel lost or rejected from the Lord when I failed Him. I knew the Father loved me (Jer. 31:3) and that He would never leave me (Deut. 31:8). I also recognized there shouldn't be anxiety in my relationship with the Lord. After all, 1 John 4:18 teaches, "There is no fear in love; but perfect love casts out fear, because fear involves punishment, and the one who fears is not perfected in love." Feeling scared all the time did not fit me as a child of God (2 Tim. 1:7).

So I began to investigate. I read, studied God's Word, and examined what Christ's sacrificial, substitutionary death on the cross really meant for each of us. Eventually, the flawed belief that I could lose my salvation absolutely crumbled under the truth of Scripture.

> *Flawed beliefs will eventually crumble under the truth of Scripture.*

Now, my purpose here is not to provide an argument for the doctrine of eternal security. I have already done so in my book *Eternal Se-*

curity, and I hope if you have questions about the permanency of your salvation, you'll read it. Rather, the point is that my erroneous understanding of God's nature was filling me with fear and shaping how I lived. I was constantly anxious that I would displease Him and lose my relationship with Him.

Perhaps you find yourself in a similar situation. Maybe you don't really trust the Lord with your future. Maybe you're uncertain that He really loves you or that He's reliable. You're not quite sure you can trust Him to provide for you or sustain you because you've already experienced so much adversity. How can you be sure that God is who He says He is? How can you be certain He really cares about you?

You do just as I did. You investigate, seek Him in prayer, study His Word, examine all He provided for you on the cross, and ask, "Lord, do I have an accurate view of who You are, how You love me, and what You are teaching me? Am I learning about You and trusting You as I should? Am I holding on to any wrong beliefs that hinder my knowing You and interacting with You?"

If you doubt the Lord's character, motives, and plan, then it is no wonder you are fearful.

If you doubt the Lord's character, motives, and plan, then it is no wonder you are fearful. In Him is true hope and safe refuge. He is the one who is all sufficient and capable of helping you with perfect power and wisdom. He is the one greater than all your difficulties and able to overcome them. And He is the one you were called to rely upon from the very beginning (Ps. 71:5–8).

Without the ability to fully trust Him, anxiety will always have a hold on you. After all, where else can you turn? Everything else fails—every other earthly defense can be overcome. As David wrote in Psalm 20:7–8, "Some boast in chariots and some in horses, but we will boast in the name of the LORD, our God. They have bowed down and fallen, but we have risen and stood upright." If you lack faith in the Father, then it is not surprising that you sometimes feel helpless and overwhelmed.

But you do not have to fear anymore. After almost seventy years of knowing Jesus as my Lord and Savior, I can honestly and gratefully say that God is more wonderfully loving, compassionate, and wise than I could ever have imagined. He has never let me down, and He will not disappoint you either.

Friend, other people may fail to act in your best interest, even when they have good intentions. But your loving Father never will—He will always do what is most beneficial for your life, even when it doesn't seem like it.

TRIUMPHING OVER ABIDING FEAR

Are you willing to try? Do you have any valid reasons to hold on to your fear when God has said you don't have to? Remember, He promises you in Isaiah 41:10, "Do not fear, for I am with you; do not anxiously look about you, for I am your God. I will strengthen you, surely I will help you, surely I will uphold you with My righteous right hand."

This means that regardless of what you are facing in life, the

Sovereign God of the universe—your omnipotent Creator, wise Father, mighty Defender, and awesome Lord—is going to hold you securely in the palm of His hand. He will provide for you, protect you, and deliver you. He will hold you safely and bring you through life's difficulties victoriously, no matter what. Therefore, choose to know Him better and trust Him more. Decide right now to overcome your fears.

How do you do so?

1. Acknowledge Your Anxiety to God

Your first step in overcoming anxiety is admitting it honestly to the Lord. Philippians 4:6–7 admonishes, "Be anxious for nothing, but in everything by prayer and supplication with thanksgiving let your requests be made known to God. And the peace of God, which surpasses all comprehension, will *guard* your hearts and your minds in Christ Jesus" (emphasis added). The word "guard" in this case is *phroureo* in Greek, which means "to garrison you about like an army, building a wall around you to protect you" from fear. In other words, when you bring your anxieties to the Lord, He helps you to understand that *He* is your safety.

God is your safety.

I cannot stress this enough: Your personal relationship with the Father is *everything*—the most important aspect of your life, without exception. It is the basis of your joy, peace, fulfillment, worth, and success. Through communion with Him, you can find answers to your questions about who He is and who He created you to be. Being on your knees in close, personal interaction with Him is how you will surely triumph over all of your fears. As I always say, your intimacy with God—His first priority for your life—determines the impact of your life. Therefore, it is crucial that your first step is to take all that you're feeling to Him.

Remember the words of Asaph, "My flesh and my heart may fail, but God is the strength of my heart and my portion forever" (Ps. 73:26). Everyone faces times of fear, but the men and women who triumph are the ones who take their troubles to the Lord, who is able to overcome them.

2. Identify the Root Causes of Your Fears and Confront Them

As we saw at the beginning of the chapter, for us to conquer our apprehensions, it is crucial we discover from where they originate, which then shows us what thoughts trigger them. So let me ask you, as you read through the possible sources of your anxiety, which stood out?

- Are there attitudes you were taught as a child that are causing you to worry?
- Has your imagination been running out of control, creating shadow fears that continually torment you?
- Has a lack of information about a situation, your relationships with God or others, or some unknowable future concern been producing feelings of unease within you?

- Is it possible that your trepidations stem from a wrong view of God's nature and character?

As you think of these sources, write down what they are and what messages they cause you to repeat to yourself. This is important because the way to overcome these roots is to replace them with God's Word.

For example, the man who never saw his father express fear would often tell himself, "Real men aren't afraid. Stop being such a sissy." These thoughts did not make anything better; rather, they made him feel like a failure. But imagine if when those thoughts began, he counteracted them by quoting Psalm 56:3: "When I am afraid, I will put my trust in You." Then, every time anxiety rose up within him, it would remind him to express His faith in the Lord. You cannot tell me that that won't eventually make a tremendous difference in his life. The Spirit of God working through the Word of God in a heart dedicated to Him will always succeed in glorifying the Father in ways you cannot even begin to imagine (Isa. 55:10–11; Heb. 4:12–16).

> *The Spirit of God working through the Word of God in a heart dedicated to Him will always succeed.*

Think about a young person who fears the future and wonders if there will be any jobs for her when she graduates. Most likely, she is thinking, *What's the use? All this studying and there will probably be no place to work. Why even try?* Such thoughts wouldn't inspire anyone to do her best—they have defeat written all over them. But suppose that every time this young lady's mind turned to the future, she disciplined herself to remember God's awesome promise in Jeremiah 29:11–13: "'I know the plans that I have for you,' declares the LORD, 'plans for welfare and not for calamity to give you a future and a hope. Then you will call upon Me and come and pray to Me, and I will listen to you. You will seek Me and find Me when you search for Me with all your heart.'" Not only will she want to do her best in anticipation and preparation for God's assignments, but she will also begin watching for His provision and direction. The Holy Spirit works through the Word of God to transform her mind and outlook (Rom. 12:2).

So write down each negative thought that comes into your mind—no matter how big or overwhelming the problem that accompanies it. Next, ask God to give you a promise from the Bible as a replacement for every destructive message you tell yourself. Memorize the verse(s). Then whenever you catch yourself thinking those harmful, fear-inducing thoughts, quote the Scripture.

3. Change Your Focus from Fear to God

Choosing Scripture to counteract the wrong thoughts within you will start you on the path to the third step, which is focusing on the Father rather than on the issue that is causing you to be anxious. You see, if you measure the adversity you're facing against your own ability to handle it, you will always experience fear. You cannot help it—no human can. The trials, worries, burdens, and concerns that arise can seem absolutely overwhelming. But when you look at them in terms of what the Sovereign Lord can do, nothing seems impossible (Ps. 103:19; Mark 10:27).

Therefore, always keep these two facts in mind:

First, the Lord loves you unconditionally and wants the best for you. The apostle Paul asks, "He who did not spare His own Son, but delivered Him over for us all, how will He not also with Him freely give us all things?" (Rom. 8:32). Do you believe the Lord would willingly sacrifice so much so that you could know Him and then leave you helpless? Of course He wouldn't.

Therefore, you don't have to wonder if the Father has your best interests at heart. He absolutely does (Jer. 29:11). You never have to fear He will abandon you because of something you've done wrong. He won't (Heb. 13:5). He says, "I have loved you with an everlasting love" (Jer. 31:3), which means you can trust He will always lead you in the best way possible.

This does not suggest that you won't have struggles that tempt you to fear and cause you to doubt. In fact, you will most likely experience adversity until you see Him face-to-face in heaven because trials and difficulties build your faith and trust in Him (1 Pet. 1:6–7). But when you encounter challenges, you can be completely certain that He's allowed them for your benefit (Rom. 8:28). You may not understand what's happening to you, but you can continue to live in confidence and victory because of His love.

Second, He has both the wisdom and power to help you. The Father is not only willing to help you but He is capable of doing so in ways you could never imagine (Eph. 3:20). God is *omnipotent* (all-powerful), *omniscient* (all-knowing), and *omnipresent* (simultaneously existing everywhere at once), which is possible because He is outside of time and all the limitations of this world. This is why the apostle Paul wrote, "I pray that you will begin to understand how incredibly great his power is to help those who believe in him. It is that same mighty power that raised Christ from the dead" (Eph. 1:19–20, TLB).

Is there anything you could face that requires more strength than was present at the resurrection or more wisdom than provided the victory over sin and death? Of course not. With such an awesome Counselor and Defender available to you, do you ever really have any cause for fear? Surely you don't. The immense support, provision, and encouragement that is available for you as a believer when you rely upon Him should fill you with faith, courage, and confidence. Truly, "All things are possible to him who believes" (Mark 9:23).

4. Give the Lord Praise and Thanks

After you have fixed your focus on God, there is only one thing left to do—declare your gratefulness that He is helping you and for all He has given. And I don't mean just during Sunday church services or your quiet time, either. Rather, instead of talking about your problems and voicing your worries to the people you know—as you might usually do—change what you say. Begin declaring your trust in God and testifying of His goodness in your conversations.

This may be a big shift for you, but there is awesome power

in praise and thanksgiving. Something amazing happens within us and in our situation when we rejoice and give God the glory regardless of our circumstances. Not only does our gratefulness honor the Father in the manner He deserves, but it also refocuses our attention on His ability to help us, releases us from anxiety, reinforces our faith, and encourages those with whom we are speaking (Col. 3:16–17).

This is the reason the apostle Paul instructed, "Rejoice always; pray without ceasing; in everything give thanks; for this is God's will for you in Christ Jesus" (1 Thess. 5:16–18). He understood the good it does your spirit and the way it exalts the Father when you place your trust in Him through praise.

An attitude of thanksgiving can turn any situation from hopeless to triumphant. We see it all throughout Scripture. As young David faced the mighty giant Goliath, he voiced his faith in God, saying, "This day the LORD will deliver you up into my hands . . . that all the earth may know that there is a God in Israel, and that all this assembly may know that the LORD does not deliver by sword or by spear; for the battle is the LORD's and He will give you into our hands" (1 Sam. 17:46–47). David's confidence in the Father's ability paved the way to victory.

Likewise, when three powerful armies attacked Judah, and God's people were left without earthly defenses, they went to their divine Defender with the spirit of joy. Second Chronicles 20 reports, King "Jehoshaphat stood and said, 'Listen to me, O Judah and inhabitants of Jerusalem, put your trust in the LORD your God and you will . . . succeed.' . . . When they began singing and praising, the LORD set ambushes against the sons of Ammon,

Moab and Mount Seir, who had come against Judah; so they were routed" (vv. 20, 22). Judah's thanksgiving was the perfect stage for God's supernatural triumph and provision.

And when Paul and Silas were unjustly beaten and thrown into the Philippian prison, they did not allow their pain or fear of the situation to cloud the reality of who they belonged to and what He had called them to do.

> *Thanksgiving was the perfect stage for God's supernatural triumph and provision.*

Instead of weeping and complaining, "Paul and Silas were praying and singing hymns of praise to God . . . and suddenly there came a great earthquake, so that the foundations of the prison house were shaken; and immediately all the doors were opened and everyone's chains were unfastened" (Acts 16:25–26). Again, their attitudes of trust and gratefulness were the perfect channel through which the Lord could work miraculously on their behalf.

It is an undeniable fact—there is freedom and power in praise. Like David, Jehoshaphat, and Paul, when you voice your faith and give God thanks in the midst of your adversity, you are not permitting your emotions or temporary circumstances to rule you. Rather, you acknowledge that the Lord is working despite what you can see and that you eagerly expect for Him to lead you to victory.

A CONTINUING FOCUS

Now please understand, none of this is a quick, one-time fix. Your worries and concerns may resurface in your life repeatedly and come to your mind often—perhaps even hourly at first. You will most likely need to repeat the four-step process I outlined above many times. It will certainly take time, perseverance, and consistency to root out the damaging attitudes, false beliefs, and shadow fears that torment you. This is absolutely normal. Just be patient with yourself and understand that this is a battle won by determination, discipline, and dedication to the Father.

Be patient with yourself and understand that this is a battle won by determination, discipline, and dedication to the Father.

And be assured—it absolutely works. I have a long-standing practice that when a particular verse stands out to me in a special way or gives me comfort through a trial, I write the date in the margin of my Bible. This encourages me greatly because as I look at those particular Scripture passages, I can recall what was happening in my life at that time, how the Father helped me through it, and how the Holy Spirit transformed my thoughts with His truth.

The best part is, the old feelings of fear that used to well up in me are absolutely gone—replaced by the deep abiding calm and "the peace . . . which surpasses all comprehension" (Phil. 4:7) that can only come from the Father. The enemies I faced at that time are no more. The difficulties have long since faded away. But the memory of His triumph remains to give me continued strength, peace, and confidence.

I have no doubt that He will do so for you as well.

|||||||||||||||||||||||||||||||||||||||||||||||||||||||||||||||||||||||||||||||||||||||||||||||||||||||||||||||||||||||||||||||||||

Father, how grateful I am for Your awesome love for me. You know all about my fears and offer me Your peace. Thank You for revealing the origination point of my fears so they can be rooted out completely. I praise You for helping me overcome the things I am afraid of and teaching me the way to victory.

Father, I recognize that the struggle I am facing today is because of my focus—which is on my problems and feelings, rather than on Your perfect provision. Therefore, Lord, please continue to draw me to Your presence, giving me strength and courage through Your Word and in prayer. Whenever I am anxious, immediately remind me to seek You. Show me the promises in Scripture that You wish to work through to strengthen my faith and transform my mind. Teach me about who You are so I can stand steadfast against these fears and declare in full confidence: "My God is wiser, more loving, and more powerful than any problem I could ever face!" Day by day, help me to place my focus on Your faithful character and unfailing principles so that I can be a person of courage and conviction, who obeys and pleases You. And train my mouth to praise You in every circumstance, Lord God. Convict me whenever I speak words of worry and defeat and help me to always glorify You with my conversation.

Thank You, Father, that I can lay down my fears on the basis of who You are and what You have promised me. You said I did not have to be afraid because You will always be with me, You will be my God, and You will strengthen and uphold me with Your righteous right hand. Truly, You are worthy of all of the honor, glory, power, and praise! My soul rests in You, Father. In Jesus' name I pray. Amen.

QUESTIONS FOR
PERSONAL REFLECTION AND GROUP STUDY

1. Are you aware of any attitudes that were formed during your childhood that may be causing you anxiety now that you are an adult?

2. Are there issues you fret about on an ongoing basis—such as a loved one getting sick, people rejecting you, or losing everything you own—that actually have no basis in reality? In what ways have you been dominated by these shadow fears?

3. When facing a problem, do you usually worry that the worst will happen? How has this hindered you from stepping out in faith?

4. Is there anything you believe about God that continuously causes you anxiety? Could it be that a lack of

information is causing your apprehensions? Are you willing to search Scripture to find out if your belief is incomplete or wrong?

5. How does your intimate relationship with God help you to overcome your worries? Why is a relationship with Jesus Christ important when considering a change of focus in your thinking?

6. What positive benefits could result from the difficult situations of your life? Name at least one thing you can praise God for, even though the circumstances surrounding it may not be best.

6

REJECTION

Overcoming the Most Painful Emotion

FROM EARLY ON IN LIFE, we are taught that not everyone is going to like us. Some people won't want to be our friends; they'll disagree with us and even stand in opposition to us. All of us have been rejected at one point or another and in various ways.

At times, we may even be disparaged openly and publically. I recall one business meeting when a man came up to the pulpit and hurled terrible accusations at me. It was a contentious time for First Baptist Atlanta, and he did not agree with how I was leading the congregation. So he accused me of stealing the church and running people off. He finished his tirade by threatening, "Stanley, if you don't watch out, you're going to get hurt!" He then forcefully backhanded me in the jaw.

Certainly, that was a moment when I didn't feel particularly loved or accepted. Although I received a great deal of support from the church, family, and friends, it was still unnerving to realize how much this man despised me simply because I did not cater to his point of view.

If you've ever experienced this kind of negative reaction from another person, you may have felt as humiliated, demoralized, and unsettled as I did—especially if the rebuke was carried out in such a public way. These feelings are, of course, a normal response, even when you are standing for godly values and beliefs. We may not want to admit that those moments of rejection affect us deeply, but they do. They strike at the core of who we are and what we believe about ourselves.

More often than not, however, it isn't the rebuke of strangers but the rejection of those closest to us that causes us the most pain and damage. For example, I once spoke with a woman who struggled terribly with feeling unloved and unwanted. She had three sisters, but she told me that one of her siblings was especially lovely—tall, with beautiful blonde hair—and was obviously her father's favorite. She and the other two sisters were, as she put it, "just girls"—short, brunette, and average looking.

> *It isn't the rebuke of strangers but the rejection of those closest to us that causes us the most pain and damage.*

"What makes you think he preferred your blond sister?" I asked.

"Well, one day, my father brought home this beautiful red dress and gave it to her, but the rest of us got nothing. He never did anything like that for us. We didn't say a word to him about it, but we always knew it was because he loved her best," she responded. That simple act had stayed with those women for decades, wounding them terribly.

"But surely your father loved you, too," I replied gently.

She shook her head with terrible sadness in her eyes. "He never said so. Not once. Not in my entire life."

In fact, this woman told me that when she received word that her father was dying, she went to visit him. She said, "I had to see him. I had to be with him during his last days. I wanted so badly for him to call my name and say he loved me. That's all I'd ever really hoped for. I thought maybe he would finally say it since it would be his last chance to do so."

But he didn't. This woman took care of him. Sat with him. Listened to him. And even begged him to say, "I love you." But he died refusing to express the three simple words that his daughter wanted so desperately to hear.

Consider what kind of profound, heartbreaking damage such rejection can do—never being told one is loved or accepted by a mother, father, or other caregiver. Imagine the devastation of being refused and discarded by someone so essential and central to one's life. Of course that would leave a terrible wound—how could it not?

THE MOST PAINFUL EMOTION

In fact, I believe rejection causes some of the most painful bondage that anyone ever experiences because it influences what you and I believe about ourselves. This is what happens: when a person or group of people—who may have been trying to hurt or control us—deems us unlovable, unfit, or worthless, we unconsciously accept that others must hold the same belief.

We may not perceive its effects. We may not think it bothers us. We may not even realize or remember that we were rejected. But when we are made to feel that we are unwanted, unloved, or unworthy of respect, we are wounded deep within our souls in a manner that acutely affects how we view ourselves, others, and God. Instinctively, we become more self-critical and begin to look for ways others may reinforce the negative thoughts we have about ourselves—at times even provoking people to reject us by acting out.

> *Rejection strikes at the foundation of our identity, distorting what we think is true about who we are and what we are worth.*

This is because rejection strikes at the foundation of our identity, distorting what we think is true about who we are and what we are worth. Why? Because of the sinful nature within us. Remember, "sin reigned in death" (Rom. 5:21), or as the *New Living Translation* phrases it: "Sin ruled over all people and brought them to death." The end goal of the sin nature is devastation (Rom. 5:12), so it is understandable that the injurious messages we hear find fertile soil in our hearts and take root. This is why it is much easier to believe the hurtful things said about us than comments that encourage or edify us. We embrace the messages that speed us along the path to destruction (Ps. 16:25) and dismiss that which reminds us we are created in the image of God (Gen. 1:26).

And the truth of the matter is, if we fail to recognize the presence of rejection in our lives and deal with it, it will continue to cause us pain and corrupt every relationship we have. Therefore, we must root out every false message of being unloved, unwanted, and unworthy that has been implanted in our lives and replace it with the truth of Scripture (Ps. 107:20).

THE CONSEQUENCES OF REJECTION

So, what are the telltale signs that you are living with rejection? Remember, just because you do not recall a specific incident does not mean it is necessarily gone. Your emotional wounds may have been formed in early childhood through events that you have no conscious memory of. And long-buried feelings of being undesirable or unwelcome may persist in affecting you because of what you continue to tell yourself. This is why it is so important to determine if any of the evidence of rejection is present in your life.

Therefore, as you did for fear, please consider the following consequences of rejection to determine if you have blind spots in your emotional life. Ask the Holy Spirit to uncover any hidden wounds you may have and be open to what He has to say to you. And, as always, write down whatever He reveals so you can unearth the thought patterns that hold you captive and replace them with the biblical truth that sets you free.

1. A Critical Focus on Yourself

Perhaps the most obvious symptom of being wounded by rejection is that you continually criticize yourself. To discern if this is a problem, listen to what you think about when frustrations or prob-

lems occur. Do you tell yourself you are stupid, ugly, or a failure? Do you doubt people will accept you or wonder if you are a burden to them? Do you compare yourself to others in the hope of feeling better about yourself? Are you constantly complaining about your appearance, weight, job performance, income, or other aspects of your life? Do you fret because you do not receive recognition from certain friends or authority figures? Are you concerned with devising ways of capturing their attention—both positive through good deeds and negative through complaining and such? If so, then you most likely feel you must reach a certain standard to be adequate, loveable, or worthy of respect, and those sentiments are driving your thought patterns.

You may even think to yourself, *If I would just measure up, the problems I am experiencing would not exist. But I am never going to be good enough—so this problem will never go away. I will never achieve my goals, and no one will ever really accept me.* If this is how you see yourself, my friend, then you are most certainly bound by the emotional wounds of rejection.

You may think, *But you don't understand. That's just who I am. I've failed in these areas of my life and there's no hope for me to be any different. Ask anyone who knows me—they agree that's who I am, and there's no changing me.*

If this is what you believe, we have identified a source of your problems; you are
measuring yourself by faulty standards—
the defective opinions of fallen humanity
rather than the holy, well-informed, and
wise view of your Creator—and doing so is

*To be free, measure
yourself by the holy,
well-informed, and wise
view of your Creator.*

destroying you. As we will discuss later in the chapter, God sees you very differently, and He knows you far better than anyone else ever could. You can be free of the bondage to rejection if you will let go of these critical thought patterns about yourself and accept His truth.

2. A Faultfinding View of Others

A second way rejection is noticeable in a person's life is when he is hard-hearted and derogatory toward others. If someone you know is easily angered and constantly criticizing people, it may very well be that a deep sense of inferiority is driving his unsympathetic attitude. You see, by condemning others, a person in bondage to rejection somehow feels better about himself—perhaps believing he looks good by comparison or that he is taking the attention off himself and diverting it to the person he is criticizing.

This very problem is why Jesus said in Matthew 7:3, "Why do you look at the speck that is in your brother's eye, but do not notice the log that is in your own eye?" It is so much easier to point out the faults of others than to look at our own failings. Yet this strategy never works to satisfy the deep longing each of us has in our hearts for true forgiveness, acceptance, and worthiness—at least, not in the long run.

I saw this firsthand in the life of my stepfather. For years I could not figure out why he acted as cruelly as he did. He would come home after work and angrily blast whoever crossed his path. It was almost as if he could not stop himself—he seemed compelled to be condemning, critical, and at times even physically violent.

Many days he would continue provoking me until we got into heated arguments. When our rough scuffles were over, I would feel terrible—guilty that I hadn't controlled my anger. He, to my surprise, would always appear just fine—as if nothing had happened. It was only much later in life, after he died, that I realized he was acting out of the rejection he had faced as a child. By putting down others, he felt better about himself. It alleviated some of the pressure he felt internally.

So ask yourself if you feel the need to be critical or negative. Do you judge others harshly in order to vindicate yourself? Is your first instinct to pick apart people when meeting them or experiencing conflicts with them?

Perhaps you are thinking, *Well, that's just my personality. I'm an analytical person.* Or, *Doesn't the Bible tell us to discern between good and evil, wise and foolish, godly and carnal? Doesn't Scripture tell us to turn a critical eye toward certain issues?*

Yes it does. But the vital difference between valid spiritual discernment and an attitude of rejection is your *mind-set* toward the object of your criticism.

As we said, the rejected person finds fault in order to feel better about himself or herself. The person censured doesn't necessarily matter to him or her. But whenever Jesus corrected people or even became angry at their actions, He did so out of love.

> *The vital difference between valid spiritual discernment and an attitude of rejection is your mind-set toward the object of your criticism.*

For example, when Jesus healed a man with a withered hand in the synagogue, many onlookers accused Him of doing work on the Sabbath—a practice forbidden by Jewish Law (Ex. 20:8–10). Mark 3:5 reports that Christ looked at them "with anger, *grieved at their hardness of heart*" (emphasis added). This is because as religious rulers and teachers, those men should have understood and expressed the mercy and compassion of the gracious God they served. But they didn't—a fact that caused Jesus great pain and sorrow because it showed how truly far their hearts were from the Father.

The Savior's criticism of the religious leaders wasn't out of hatred or to prove His superiority. Rather, it was out of His love for them—because they were missing the great joy of being rightly related to the Lord, and even worse, they were leading others astray as well. You can see the deep grief this caused Him when He said, "Jerusalem, Jerusalem, who kills the prophets and stones those who are sent to her! How often I wanted to gather your children together, the way a hen gathers her chicks under her wings, and you were unwilling" (Matt. 23:37).

Christ's attitude is very different from the faultfinding that comes from the person exhibiting the bondage of rejection. This is why it is always important to evaluate your motives when making judgments about others. Your rebuke may show that you are struggling with your own feelings of being unwanted and unworthy.

3. An Avoidance of Intimacy

Another way people reveal their struggle with this painful emotion is that they find it very difficult to be open and caring toward others. Why is this?

First, because of ever-present feelings of shame and low self-esteem, the person struggling with rejection may be afraid that the people she really cares about will get close enough to discover the truth—that there are thoughts and feelings deep within her that make her unlovable. In other words, she simply doesn't feel worthy of another person's love. So when this individual begins to feel people becoming too familiar or dependent, she pushes them away—sabotaging the relationship.

She may distance herself by retreating emotionally or by attempting to repel her loved ones with negative behavior. But when her friends or family members finally give up trying to break through her relational barriers, she feels vindicated in her belief that she was right to protect herself. Thus she perpetuates the cycle of rejection repeatedly, reinforcing her notion that she does not deserve another's acceptance.

Second, because of feelings of unworthiness, the person struggling with rejection may be suspicious of anyone who claims to care about him. Remember, when a person is in bondage to this painful emotion, he has trouble accepting the edifying messages spoken about him because they contradict what he believes about himself. Therefore, he may not only discard the encouragement he receives as unreliable information but he may likewise question the motives of those trying to build him up.

Consequently, he cannot receive a compliment or affection without asking, *What does this person really want from me?* Unfortunately, it is impossible to achieve intimacy with such a distrustful attitude toward others.

Third, because of hypersensitivity to cues that reinforce her negative beliefs about herself, a person struggling with rejection finds it difficult to love others because she is always looking for verification of her own lack of worth. This means that not only will she be very easily hurt but she will also be focused inward—more interested in preserving herself than being a blessing to her loved ones.

Yet we know from 1 Corinthians 13:5–7 that real, sacrificial, godly love "is not provoked, does not take into account a wrong suffered, does not rejoice in unrighteousness, but rejoices with the truth; bears all things, believes all things, hopes all things, endures all things." Or as the *Living Bible* paraphrases it, "Love does not demand its own way. It is not irritable or touchy. It does not hold grudges and will hardly even notice when others do it wrong" (v. 5).

> *True unconditional love is sacrificial—it is not easily offended, self-focused, or afraid of rejection. It seeks only the good of the other person.*

In other words, true unconditional love is sacrificial—it is not easily offended, self-focused, or afraid of rejection. It seeks only the good of the other person. We see this best in Christ's example. As the Roman soldiers beat Him, taunted Him unmercifully, and even as they drove the nails into His hands and feet, He said, "Father, forgive them; for they do not know what they are doing" (Luke 23:34). Rather than dwelling on how they were hurting *Him*, Jesus remained focused on His loving purpose for *them*—to provide forgiveness as their Savior (Rom. 5:8).

It is not possible to be inwardly focused and easily offended and truly care for others with the unconditional love Jesus teaches us to have. The tendency to protect oneself will always thwart the true openness and intimacy needed. As Jesus said, "Greater love has no one than this, that one lay down his life for his friends" (John 15:13). If you cannot even lay down your inadequacies and defenses for your loved ones, laying down your life is most likely not an option.

Finally, because he sees people as objects to be used for pleasure and never fully engages emotionally, he may feel so devalued in himself that he forgoes true intimacy for the immediate and destructive gratification of sex outside of marriage. Sadly, there are terrible consequences associated with such a practice. The feelings of shame and disconnection that arise from engaging in immoral acts cause the individual to detach from God and others even further. Because of this, he will sink deeper into a prison of isolation and rejection.

So consider: Are you ever afraid that the people you care about will get too close and find you unlovable? Are you suspicious of those who claim to care about you? Are you overly sensitive to what people say or how they act toward you? Are you more comfortable engaging with others physically than emotionally? Do you find it difficult to be open and caring toward others because you don't really feel worthy of love? If so, then this is evidence that roots of rejection are present in your life.

4. An Inclination Toward Isolation

Psychologically, rejection and loneliness are very similar because they both involve the feelings of being emotionally disconnected and the fear of being unwanted. Whereas rejection stems from another's refusal to be involved with us, loneliness often arises from our inability—because of social skill, circumstances, time, or distance—to reach out and connect with others. As you can imagine, these two emotions are closely related—once one takes root, the other frequently follows.

This is because a person who struggles with rejection often experiences difficulty in establishing genuine give-and-take friendships with others and may feel as if no one truly wants or understands her. To avoid the pain of feeling unwelcome, she may either intentionally or unconsciously separate herself from others—spending a great deal of time alone or participating in activities that do not require her to engage in meaningful ways with other people. Such isolation eventually causes the individual even deeper loneliness and bondage.

Conversely, a person who spends a great deal of time alone—and thereby does not have opportunities to practice interacting with others—may be misunderstood as aloof, awkward, or detached in social situations, which then elicits undesirable and adverse reactions from her peers. When such negative interactions occur, feelings of inadequacy and rejection can develop and more wounding can occur.

However, regardless of whether the rejection or loneliness comes first, the result is increasing alienation and isolation—and that is never a good thing.

This is a difficulty that hits especially close to home for me because I have faced profound loneliness in my life. In fact, one of my earliest memories is from a very painful experience. I was a small boy— only two or three years old. I recall that I had a terrible earache, but there was no one to take care of me because Mother had to work. So I sat alone on the bed in our little wooden house, crying—with only a dim kerosene lamp to keep me company. I felt like no one would ever come help me.

I felt like no one would ever come help me.

Another early memory is of coming home to an empty house after school. I was in the first grade, and I can still remember the long black key that we hid under a brick outside. Only Mother and I knew where it was. As I would turn that key in the lock and open the door, I would often think to myself, *I'm going to be all alone.*

I'm going to be all alone.

Although I knew my mother was doing her best to provide for me, I still remember feeling terribly insecure in that house all by myself.

Likewise, I vividly recall one Saturday afternoon long ago

when two of my friends—Rob and Jimmy—came to spend some time with me. We were laughing and playing games when sud-

denly one of the boys' father came to pick them up in his car. As I stood in the yard and watched the three of them drive away without me, a sinking feeling hit me in the pit of my stomach. I clearly

I have no one.

remember thinking, *I have no one.* In that moment, I had the feeling of utter, devastating loneliness. I felt rejected, as if there was no one in the world I could count on as a friend.

Have you ever felt this way—as if you were alone in the world with no one to help you? As if you would always be alone? As if you had absolutely no one? It's a horrible thing to face. Maybe, like me, you felt isolated as a young child. Or perhaps your feelings of alienation came later in life. You may even be struggling right now with how to find friends and develop meaningful, supportive relationships.

Loneliness is a very painful emotion that all of us experience at one point or another. However, if we don't deal with our feelings of alienation, the wounds of rejection will deepen, and more destructive attitudes will eventually develop.

In fact, because such isolation is so devastating, the enemy will do all he can to intensify it—even using shame and fear to drive you deeper into hiding. Therefore, if you struggle with loneliness and rejection, you may face an overwhelming temptation to camouflage your sadness and disconnectedness from others and distance yourself from them further. Don't do it. No Christian has ever been called to "go it alone" in his or her walk of faith. The

Father created you for relationship and calls you to live in meaningful fellowship with other believers (Heb. 10:24–25). Therefore, acknowledge your loneliness to God and trust Him to help you overcome it.

5. A Preoccupation with Image and Counterfeit Measures of Worth

A final indication that a person is struggling with feeling unworthy is an excessive emphasis on outward factors that will gain him approval or attention. How does this manifest itself in his life?

First, a person may be overly concerned about his appearance. Perhaps he believes that if he dresses better—with more expensive or stylish clothes—he will receive the attention of others and win their admiration and respect. If he can just give the impression of importance and worth outwardly, then perhaps others will believe he is truly significant and worthwhile.

This does not mean that it is wrong for a person to dress well, exercise, eat right, and feel good about his appearance. In fact, I often say, "Look your best, do your best, and be your best, because that is life at its best." Rather, the problem is when appearance becomes an all-consuming preoccupation. We often see the outliers of this in the media with people who become addicted to plastic surgery, advocate extreme diets, or who pursue unnatural standards of fitness. But a fixation on one's looks and dress can be evident in subtle ways, too, and it can become a terrible trap.

For example, I recall one morning after a church service I saw a friend, smiled, and said, "You look fantastic today!"

Rather than say, "Thank you," the person responded, *"Today?* Didn't you like how I looked last Sunday? What? Is this the first time you've ever seen me appearing presentable?" The reaction shocked me. But I came away from that encounter recognizing that preoccupation with image can place a person in bondage. At all times the person's antennae are up, waiting for any sign that his or her self-criticism is warranted.

Second, a person may try to prove her superiority through possessions and achievements. A person in bondage to rejection may believe that if she has a fine car, an expensive house, all the latest gadgets, or a prominent job, people will think she is someone of importance in this world. So she masks how badly she struggles with inferiority by focusing on the surface issues of wealth and social standing.

Sadly, this never works to build a person's sense of worth. Earthly goods and power can never fill one's emptiness, give self-esteem, or restore dignity. And the more a person flaunts her belongings and accomplishments to prove she is worthy of being loved, the more she will be perceived by others as superficial and arrogant. Furthermore, such a lifestyle requires a tremendous outflow of money to maintain—sometimes far beyond the person's ability to earn it.

> *Earthly goods and power can never fill one's emptiness, give self-esteem, or restore dignity.*

This, of course, exacerbates her feelings of being out of control and living a lie.

Third, a person may become prone to perfectionism—believing he must appear absolutely faultless in order to be accepted. This is a form of enslavement that comes from a person finding his value in his ability to perform. A perfectionist tends to be afraid of admitting any faults—because doing so would devalue him. So he strives to master and control every aspect of his life. Often, this means setting unreasonable standards that are impossible to reach or maintain. To avoid failure, he may refuse to attempt any task he cannot accomplish perfectly. He may also procrastinate in carrying out important assignments if he is fearful that he cannot do them well enough.

Again, if you see any evidence of these factors in your life, it is likely you have deeply ingrained rejection. Friend, you do not have to look a certain way, have a lot of money or success, or be perfect in your performance in order to be loved. In fact, your attempts to prove your worth may actually be turning people away.

ROOTING OUT REJECTION

When we experience rejection, we may do all sorts of things to feel better about ourselves, soothe our pain, or try to prove our worth. But as you can see, our ways don't always bring us the results we hope for. In fact, our strategies for dealing with our feelings of rejection may be downright destructive and cause us to miss God's best for our lives. What, then, can we do to overcome this terribly painful emotion?

The only way to have victory over rejection is to release the damaging ideas we have about ourselves and take hold of God's truth.

The only way to have victory over rejection is to release the damaging ideas we have about ourselves and take hold of God's truth.

Friend, there is only one Person who knows your true significance and potential—and that is the One who knit you together in your mother's womb (Ps. 139:13–16). Only He understands what is in your heart and what is possible for your future (1 Sam. 16:7; Jer. 29:11). Only He is worthy of judging your value and can set you free from the false messages that keep you in bondage (Heb. 4:12–13). That one is the triune God, who loves you without measure—the Father who created you, the Lord Jesus who saves you, and the Holy Spirit who indwells you (1 Pet. 1:1–2).

There is no need to go through life handicapped by past experiences. What others say about you doesn't matter. How they treated you is inconsequential. The only accurate, eternal, unassailable measure of your worth comes from almighty God, who will one day judge the living and the dead without exception (1 Pet. 4:4–5). And through Scripture He reveals the three indispensable aspects of your personhood you need in order to escape the bondage of rejection. They are:

- A sense of belonging—of being part of something important.
- A feeling of worthiness—of being valuable.
- A recognition of competence—of being capable.

Thankfully, not only does the Father tell us what we need, He also fulfills all the requirements so that we may feel fully accepted, worthy, and competent. So as you read, embrace the truth of who you really are because of His great provision.

1. Belonging Through God's Adoption

Whenever you are burdened with feelings of rejection, one of the first things you must do is remember your adoption as a child of God (Gal. 4:4–7). As a believer in Jesus Christ, you can be absolutely certain that your loving heavenly Father has chosen you, accepts you as His child, and wants to be part of your life. The apostle Paul testifies, "You have received a spirit of adoption as sons by which we cry out, 'Abba! Father!' The Spirit Himself testifies with our spirit that we are children of God, and if children, heirs also, heirs of God and fellow heirs with Christ" (Rom. 8:15–17). You must embrace this as a fact: *The Father loves you and rejoices in calling you His own.*

You must embrace this as a fact: The Father loves you and rejoices in calling you His own.

Does He agree with everything you do? Not necessarily. Is He disappointed when you sin? Yes. But is there anything in this world that you can do to make Him care for you any less? Absolutely not. The Lord loves you fully, unconditionally, and sacrificially—more than you can possibly imagine. He knows every unfitting thought in your mind and every unpleasant meditation of your heart. He realizes your faults, shortcomings, limitations, physical imperfections, relational weaknesses, and emotional deficiencies. He sees all of it more deeply than anyone else ever could. And He still sacrificed everything so you could spend eternity with Him because He could not bear to be parted from you (Rom. 5:8). Absolutely nothing can separate you from His love (Rom. 8:38–39) or remove you from His sovereign hand (John 10:27–29).

Now, why is it important to understand this first? Because, as we've discussed, at times it is very difficult to pinpoint the source of our emotions of rejection. Sometimes we know exactly what caused our feelings of pain—such as divorce, betrayal, dismissal from a job, failed promotions, broken relationships, or some other easily identifiable incident or group of events. But more often than not, we may have experienced abandonment or losses as children that we do not remember. Likewise, we may not realize that certain events in our lives have affected us in such a devastating manner.

As I said in Chapter 4, I lost my own father at nine months of age, and it had an incredible impact on me. Throughout my life it was very difficult to define why I experienced such profound emptiness and uncertainty. My father had not deserted or rejected me in the literal sense, but his absence through death had the same impact on my young heart as outright rejection would—creating feelings of being unloved and insecure. Similarly, you do not need to hear negative words to feel unwanted or unloved. You could have developed those feelings by a parent's absence or emotional distance.

Most parents have no idea how easy it is to set their child in the wrong direction very early in life. Any time a caregiver says by their words or actions, "I don't have time for you," the person hearing that message may interpret it, in part, as, "You are not worthy of my time or my love." And it takes only one devastating statement or one terrible event to wound our hearts for life. This acute vulnerability is simply who we are as fallen humanity.

This is why it is so important to embrace how God sees us. We must start building our identities anew from the understanding that *He wants us* and invites us to *belong to His family*. Understanding that He desires a relationship with us and always accepts us is the balm that can heal our wounds no matter where they originate.

> *We must start building our identities anew from the understanding that He wants us and invites us to belong to His family.*

This is why the concept of adoption should be so meaningful to us as believers. Ephesians 1:4–6 tells us, "He chose us in Him before the foundation of the world, that we would be holy and blameless before Him. In love He predestined us to adoption as sons through Jesus Christ to Himself, according to the kind intention of His will, to the praise of the glory of His grace, which He freely bestowed on us in the Beloved."

It is God's will that our bond to Him be the strongest it can be, so He bestows on us the most precious relationship possible—He accepts us as His children. He intentionally draws us to Himself—choosing us to know Him, experience His salvation, and spend eternity with Him. He does not save us because He *has* to; He redeems us because He *desires* to have a deep, meaningful relationship with us.

Additionally we should note that adoption was a very serious matter in the Roman Empire. A parent might be able to disown a natural child, but not one he had legally chosen through adoption to bear the full rights of a member of the family. In other words, we will never be abandoned or ignored by our heavenly Father—His commitment to us is authentic and eternally binding (Eph. 1:13–14). In fact, He seals us with His Holy Spirit as a constant reminder that He will make good on His promises to us (2 Cor. 1:21–22). Knowing this and confident that understanding this truth can help free you from the bondage to rejection, I echo the apostle Paul's prayer for you and all believers:

I bow my knees before the Father, from whom every family in heaven and on earth derives its name, that He would grant you, according to the riches of His glory, to be strengthened with power through His Spirit in the inner man, so that Christ may dwell in your hearts through faith; and that you, being rooted and grounded in love, may be able to comprehend with all the saints what is the breadth and length and height and depth, and to know the love of Christ which surpasses knowledge, that you may be filled up to all the fullness of God. (Ephesians 3:14–19)

I also pray that when you have feelings of rejection, you will remind yourself of the reality of who you are. You are the chosen child of the King of Kings and the Lord of Lords. You are not an outcast or misfit. You are not unlovable or defective. You are not alone in this world. You are known completely and loved unconditionally. You belong to God's family permanently and, as such, are an important part of His holy and wonderful presence in the world.

2. *Worth Through a Relationship with Christ*

A second place where we suffer from the wounds of rejection is in our sense of value—we struggle with feeling worthy of love and respect. We look at our faults, imperfections, and failures and wonder how others could possibly care about us. The Lord answers this need by pointing to the most significant and costly sacrifice made for anyone throughout history: Christ's death on the cross.

In Romans 8:31–34 the apostle Paul testifies,

> If God is for us, who is against us? He who did not spare His own Son, but delivered Him over for us all, how will He not also with Him freely give us all things? Who will bring a charge against God's elect? God is the one who justifies; who is the one who condemns? Christ Jesus is He who died, yes, rather who was raised, who is at the right hand of God, who also intercedes for us.

In other words, the one Person with the authority to judge your value—who owns and rules everything in all Creation—made this

eternal assessment: *You are worth dying for.* You are worth pur-
chasing with His own blood. Therefore,
no one else has any right to condemn
you or to question your significance. Not
even you.

The one Person with the
authority to judge your
value—who owns and
rules everything in all
Creation—made this
eternal assessment: You
are worth dying for.

Of course, that wasn't all the Lord
gave you through salvation. As a member of God's family, you are a coheir
with Jesus, which means He has given
you many wonderful gifts and privi-
leges. In fact, Ephesians 1:3 tells us,
"Blessed be the God and Father of
our Lord Jesus Christ, who has blessed us with *every spiritual*
blessing in the heavenly places *in Christ*" (emphasis added).
Not only are you worthy because He died for you, you are
also of immeasurable value because you have been placed "in
Christ" and everything that is His has been conferred to you
(Eph. 1:18–23).

What have you received? What does Scripture say is true about
you when you accept Jesus as your Lord and Savior? There are
more, of course, but here are fifty facts about you that represent
how the Father sees you:

1. You are a new creation (2 Cor. 5:17).
2. You are a child of the almighty, sovereign God
   (Rom. 8:16).
3. You are born again to a living hope (1 Pet. 1:23).
4. You are alive with Christ (Eph. 2:5).

5. You are the Lord's heir and a co-heir with Christ of His great kingdom (Rom. 8:17).

6. You are the righteousness of God in Christ (2 Cor. 5:21).

7. You are indwelt by the Holy Spirit (1 Cor. 3:16).

8. You are a temple of the living God (2 Cor. 6:16).

9. You are conformed to Christ's matchless likeness (Rom. 8:29).

10. You are unconditionally loved (1 John 3:1).

11. You are permanently forgiven (Eph. 1:7).

12. You are eternally redeemed (Gal. 3:13).

13. You are liberated from all condemnation (Rom. 8:1).

14. You are holy and blameless (Col. 1:22).

15. You are free (Gal. 5:1).

16. You are safe (John 10:28–29).

17. You are comforted (2 Cor. 1:3–4).

18. You are blessed with every spiritual blessing, which no one can earn on his own (Eph. 1:3).

19. You are a saint (1 Cor. 1:2).

20. You are called, justified, and glorified (Rom. 8:30).

21. You are a chosen race, a royal priesthood, a holy nation, and God's own possession (1 Pet. 2:9).

22. You are a minister of reconciliation (2 Cor. 5:19).

23. You are an ambassador for Christ (2 Cor. 5:20).

24. You are the salt of the earth (Matt. 5:13).

25. You are the light of the world (Matt. 5:14).

26. You are a fisher of men (Matt. 4:19).

27. You are the Body of Christ (1 Cor. 12:27).

28. You are God's handiwork created for good works (Eph. 2:10).

29. You are equipped and instructed (2 Tim. 3:16–17).

30. You are empowered (Phil. 4:13).

31. You are perfected, confirmed, strengthened, and established (1 Pet. 5:10).

32. You are a partaker of His divine nature (2 Peter 1:4).

33. You have peace with God (Rom. 5:1).

34. You have eternal life (John 3:16).

35. You have access to the throne of grace (Heb. 4:16).

36. You have an attentive and loving Father (Matt. 7:11).

37. You have a firm foundation (Luke 6:47–48).

38. You have provision for all your needs (Phil. 4:19).

39. You have purpose (Matt. 5:16).

40. You have a mission (Matt. 28:19–20).

41. You have a support system (Heb. 10:24–25).

42. You have the mind of Christ (1 Cor. 2:16).

43. You have the fruit of the Spirit: love, joy, peace, patience, kindness, goodness, faithfulness, gentleness, and self-control (Gal. 5:22–23).

44. You have spiritual gifts (1 Tim. 4:14).

45. You have a hope that does not disappoint (Rom. 5:5).

46. You have victory (1 Cor. 15:57).

47. You have a home in heaven (John 14:2).

48. You have an imperishable promise (1 Cor. 15:50–54).

49. You have an unshakable kingdom (Heb. 12:8).

50. You have a secure future—your name written permanently in His book of life (Rev. 3:5).

Of course, there is a great deal more you can learn about your identity as a believer in Scripture. But the point is, you have immeasurable worth through your relationship with Christ. This is a fact.

Now, I realize that such information may be difficult for you to receive because of the wounds in your heart. If you have never known the unconditional love of a godly father or have always been forced to defend yourself and find your own way, it may be especially difficult. But like the gift of salvation, you must accept all of this truth by faith—with "the assurance of things hoped for, the conviction of things not seen" (Heb. 11:1). You must choose to believe these facts about your personhood.

I say this to you because I have been where you are right now. Again, as I said in Chapter 4, for years I struggled to embrace the reality that God really cared about me because I simply could not feel His love. Intellectually I knew He loved me, but emotionally He felt distant and detached. I wanted to experience His caring presence, but the more I tried to sense it, the more separated from Him I felt.

During those days when my four friends helped me discover the source of my disconnection from God, one of the men counseled me in a way that changed my life. He encouraged me to say aloud every night, "Thank You, heavenly Father, for loving me."

At first, I felt like doing so was a little disingenuous. I asked, "Am I lying when I say that? God knows I struggle with feeling His love."

He replied, "No, you are simply stating what is true. God does

Speak truth into your heart in order to help your soul receive what the Father has for you.

love you. You are merely speaking truth to your own heart and mind and developing a way for your soul to receive what the Father has for you."

It took about six months of saying, "Thank You, heavenly Father, for loving me," before I could feel His love really take root in the core of my being. But when it did, what a glorious freedom I felt. What I had been saying became reality in my emotions, and I had a new sense of confidence and self-worth.

Of course, you may be thinking, *Well, I've tried repeating the truth to myself. It does not work.* Yes it does—I have seen the effectiveness of it myself. But here is the problem: The rejection you've experienced is entrenched deep within you with untold tentacles of woundedness and strongholds of defense surrounding it. These forces do not let go easily. In fact, it may even be quite painful for you as those destructive messages are dislodged from your heart because of how deeply intertwined they have become with your identity. There is no quick fix. It takes time and the Spirit of God working in you to heal the wounds you bear. You must give yourself a chance to form a new pattern of thinking—and that will require that you exhibit endurance, discipline, and determination as the Father teaches you how to be freed from your bondage.

So as you read God's Word, make note of what you have been given "in Christ" (2 Cor. 1:20, NLT) and accept all the Father has created you to be and enjoy. You do not have to prove your worth and you certainly do not have to accept others' assessments of your value. You are a coheir with Christ, and your inheritance is the kingdom of the living God. Be patient with yourself. Forgive your failures as He does. And continue embracing His unassailable truth that you are worthy and have great value.

3. Competence Through the Holy Spirit

So far, we have addressed two of the core questions of rejection. The first is, *Who has a right to reject us?* The answer, of course, is that no one does because God—the only One with the authority to judge us—has accepted us for all of eternity. We *belong* to the Father. He has adopted us as His own children and made us a permanent part of His family.

The second question is, *On what basis could another person reject us?* Again, any reason for you to be spurned was destroyed at the cross. Christ Himself has declared you *worthy* and has given you every spiritual blessing.

But there is a third question that is likely to plague us even when the first two are answered, and that is the issue of ability: *What if another rejects me because I am incapable of performing as he or she expects?*

This is often where the enemy attacks us with the greatest ferocity because it is so easy for him to make our trials and burdens appear insurmountable and our abilities seem insignificant. If he can discourage us, he can paralyze us from moving forward. And if he can stop us—reinforcing our feelings of inadequacy and failure—he knows he's defeated us. You know the messages that play in your mind when he attacks:

How am I going to handle such a terribly immense challenge?

There is absolutely no way! I feel so inadequate and inferior. I have nothing. I'm stupid. I'm useless. I'm weak and worthless. No wonder people forget I exist. It should come as no surprise that I have no one I can count on. After all, no one really loves me or possibly ever could.

In fact, most of the time I feel like everyone hates me—even God. No one will help me. I have no one I can trust. No one ever stands up for me. I guess I'm just not strong, smart, or attractive enough for anyone to care about me. Even my parents didn't want me. They made it clear that I was a mistake. Well, I guess I can't really blame anyone for rejecting me—I even despise myself. I'm such a failure. I deserve to be alone.

Does any of that sound familiar? Friend, you must recognize that these destructive messages are from the enemy. They are not true. They are not your reality.

Rather, the truth is that the Lord will enable you to do anything He calls you to do. So whenever the thought *What if I am incapable of performing as so-and-so expects?* crosses your mind, you can say with confidence, "There is only one I really have to please, and that is my heavenly Father." And like the apostle Paul, you can testify, "I can do all things through Him who strengthens me" (Phil. 4:13). The Lord has promised that He will never let you down and you can count on it—He never will (Josh. 1:9; 21:45).

> *The Lord will enable you to do anything He calls you to do.*

Therefore, as a child of the living God who has the Holy Spirit living within you, recognize that you are supremely equipped, empowered, and able to do all He has planned for you. He will be with you to handle whatever circumstances may come into your life. In fact, the Lord placed you in this specific environment at this unique time in history so you could fulfill a very special role in His unfolding plan for the ages (Acts 17:26–28). He has great things to accomplish through you and has every confidence that you are the right person for the job.

So discover the Father's attitude about you and claim it. Repeat it to yourself. Get it into your heart and mind. Because it is only when you are able to replace the enemy's lie with His truth that you will be able to cast off your bondage to rejection, experience life at its very best, and be His vessel of triumph in the world.

THE ENEMY'S LIE	GOD'S TRUTH— OUR DEFENSE
There is absolutely no way for me to handle such a terribly immense challenge.	I can do all things through Him who strengthens me. —PHILIPPIANS 4:13
I feel so inadequate and inferior.	Our adequacy is from God, who also made us adequate as servants of a new covenant, not of the letter but of the Spirit; for the letter kills, but the Spirit gives life. —2 CORINTHIANS 3:5–6

THE ENEMY'S LIE	GOD'S TRUTH— OUR DEFENSE
I have nothing.	My God will supply all your needs according to His riches in glory in Christ Jesus. —PHILIPPIANS 4:19
I am so stupid.	Let the name of God be blessed forever and ever, for wisdom and power belong to Him. . . . He gives wisdom to wise men and knowledge to men of understanding. It is He who reveals the profound and hidden things. —DANIEL 2:20–22
I am useless.	To each one is given the manifestation of the Spirit for the common good. —1 CORINTHIANS 12:7

THE ENEMY'S LIE	GOD'S TRUTH— OUR DEFENSE
I am weak and worthless.	He has said to me, "My grace is sufficient for you, for power is perfected in weakness." Most gladly, therefore, I will rather boast about my weaknesses, so that the power of Christ may dwell in me. Therefore I am well content with weaknesses, with insults, with distresses, with persecutions, with difficulties, for Christ's sake; for when I am weak, then I am strong. —2 CORINTHIANS 12:9–10

THE ENEMY'S LIE	GOD'S TRUTH— OUR DEFENSE
No wonder people forget I exist.	Can a woman forget her nursing child and have no compassion on the son of her womb? Even these may forget, but I will not forget you. Behold, I have inscribed you on the palms of My hands. —ISAIAH 49:15–16
I have no one I can count on.	I know the LORD is always with me. I will not be shaken, for he is right beside me. No wonder my heart is glad, and I rejoice. My body rests in safety. —PSALM 16:8–9, NLT
No one really loves me or possibly ever could.	The LORD appeared . . . saying, "I have loved you with an everlasting love; therefore I have drawn you with loving-kindness." —JEREMIAH 31:3

THE ENEMY'S LIE	GOD'S TRUTH— OUR DEFENSE
I feel like everyone hates me— even God.	Neither death, nor life, nor angels, nor principalities, nor things present, nor things to come, nor powers, nor height, nor depth, nor any other created thing, will be able to separate us from the love of God, which is in Christ Jesus our Lord. —ROMANS 8:38–39
No one will help me.	God is our refuge and strength, always ready to help in times of trouble. So we will not fear. —PSALM 46:1–2, NLT

THE ENEMY'S LIE	GOD'S TRUTH— OUR DEFENSE
I have no one I can trust.	The LORD is my strength and my shield; my heart trusts in Him, and I am helped; therefore my heart exults, and with my song I shall thank Him. —PSALM 28:7
No one ever stands up for me.	If God is for us, who is against us? . . . in all these things we overwhelmingly conquer through Him who loved us. —ROMANS 8:31, 37
I'm just not strong, smart, or attractive enough for anyone to care about me.	"Not by might nor by power, but by My Spirit," says the LORD of hosts. —ZECHARIAH 4:6

THE ENEMY'S LIE	GOD'S TRUTH— OUR DEFENSE
Even my parents didn't want me.	You have always been my helper . . . O God of my salvation! Even if my father and mother abandon me, the LORD will hold me close. —PSALM 27: 9–10, NLT
It is clear that I was a mistake.	For You formed my inward parts; You wove me in my mother's womb. . . . Your eyes have seen my unformed substance; and in Your book were all written the days that were ordained *for me*, when as yet there was not one of them. —PSALM 139:13, 16

THE ENEMY'S LIE	GOD'S TRUTH— OUR DEFENSE
I can't really blame anyone for rejecting me—I even despise myself.	I will give thanks to You, for I am fearfully and wonderfully made; wonderful are Your works, and my soul knows it very well. —PSALM 139:14
I'm such a failure.	Thanks be to God, who gives us the victory through our Lord Jesus Christ. —1 CORINTHIANS 15:57
I deserve to be alone.	The LORD is the one who goes ahead of you; He will be with you. He will not fail you or forsake you. Do not fear or be dismayed. —DEUTERONOMY 31:8

TURNING REJECTION AROUND: THE HEALING POWER OF LOVE

Just one more thing needs to be said as we conclude this important topic. Rejection is a difficult wound to heal, to be sure, but it is often made much worse if you insist on winning the approval of the people who don't care about you. First, this is because the people who've made you feel unwanted might not know how to express the acceptance you desire. Often people wound us out of their own feelings of unworthiness and alienation and do not recognize how to respond to us in a way that would build us up.

But the second reason you should beware of seeking their love is this: you are looking in the wrong direction. As long as you continue to focus on those who have rejected you to fill your needs, you will be intensely conscious of your own lack of love and the pain it causes. The Bible, however, teaches you to fix your attention in a different direction. In Luke 6:35–38, Jesus instructs,

"Love your enemies, and do good, and lend, expecting nothing in return; and your reward will be great, and you will be sons of the Most High; for He Himself is kind to ungrateful and evil men. Be merciful, just as your Father is merciful. Do not judge, and you will not be judged; and do not condemn, and you will not be condemned; pardon, and you will be pardoned. Give, and it will be given to you. They will pour into your lap a good measure—pressed down, shaken together, and running over. For by your standard of measure it will be measured to you in return."

In other words, not only is it important that you focus on God, who accepts you freely, but it is also crucial to turn your attention outward from *your* desires to the needs of *others*. You are to love those whom God gives you to care for—whether they return your affection or not.

Love those whom God gives you to care for— whether they return your affection or not.

The words "I love you" are powerful—both for those who hear them and for those who express them. I have seen God work through them in a powerful way to change people's lives. They certainly did for my favorite uncle, Jack.

Jack was a wonderful man. When my mother, Rebecca, got older and needed assistance, he moved to Atlanta and took care of her. I was very grateful for him and always told him so. Unfortunately, he didn't think much of himself growing up and had a difficult time accepting that people truly appreciated and respected him. He always kept his distance. When his wife died, he retreated further, feeling as if even God were rejecting him.

I would often say, "Jack, I just love you."

But he would always respond, "Now Charles, no you don't. You don't really love me."

I'd counter, "Oh, yes, I really do love you, Uncle Jack. And I'm thankful for the many ways you take such good care of Mother."

He'd just walk away, shaking his head. No matter what I said, he could not believe I genuinely cared for him. It was as if he thought, *Why would you love me? What about me could be worth*

*loving? I'm a nobody. I don't have anything. I don't deserve for any-
one to care about me.*

But I wasn't going to give up. I just kept thinking, *I'm going to
keep praying, and one of these days I'm going to get through to him.*

I can still recall exactly where I was standing when it finally
happened. It was about three years after Uncle Jack came to Atlanta, and as always, I said, "Jack, I just love you."

And he replied, "Charles, I love you, too."

To this day it brings tears to my eyes to remember it, because
once he was able to overcome his feelings of rejection, everything
about him changed. He even started hugging me! As soon as he
stopped depriving himself of the love, admiration, and respect
people wanted to show him, he became a totally different person—one who experienced true acceptance and joy.

God worked through the love I expressed to my uncle to heal
his woundedness. But the Lord also blessed me immeasurably
in the process. He grew my affection for Jack in amazing ways
and taught me a great deal about the awesome power of His divine, sacrificial love. Specifically, He showed me that the more
lavishly we care for others without expecting anything from
them in return, the more the Father pours His own love into
our hearts. Truly, "It is more blessed to give than to receive"
(Acts 20:35).

The Lord will teach you this awesome principle, too. So stop
analyzing whether or not people are rejecting you, and make it
your goal to show the love of God to whosoever you meet. Not
only will this help you heal from your bondage to rejection, but
the Father will work through you to bring freedom to others as

well. Go to Him in prayer, thanking Him for the work He is doing in you and asking Him to use you in the lives of others.

Father, how grateful I am for Your Holy Spirit and precious Word, which You use to set me free from my pain and suffering. Thank You for always loving me and never giving up on me. It is a great comfort to know You will never leave or forsake me.

Lord, You know the wounds of rejection that have marred my heart. You know how useless, helpless, and worthless I feel when yet another person casts me away. Many of these feelings originated long ago and have deep roots. But I am so grateful for how You set me free from these feelings. Thank You for giving me a sense of belonging in Your eternal, heavenly family as Your own beloved child. Thank You for blessing me with a sense of worthiness through Your death on the cross and resurrection. And thank You for filling me with the sense of competence and adequacy—empowering me to accomplish all You call me to through Your indwelling Holy Spirit.

Father, I must make a decision: Either I will believe what others have spoken about me or I will trust what You say about my character and future. I know You are real and that what You say counts in eternity, Lord—so I will choose to listen to You. Thank You for Your unfailing love and for creating me as You chose to—with a good plan and purpose.

Help me to keep my eyes on You and to love whosoever You send to me to care for. May everyone I come in contact with feel Your love and praise Your holy name.
In Jesus' name I pray. Amen.

QUESTIONS FOR
PERSONAL REFLECTION AND GROUP STUDY

1. How have memories of condemnation and criticism from your childhood continued to affect your relationships now as an adult?

2. Do you recognize any of the symptoms of rejection in your life? How have they manifested themselves in your relationships and daily interactions with others?

3. In what ways have you tried to release damaging ideas about yourself in order to escape the bondage of rejection? Has it worked? Why or why not?

4. Have you recognized God's desire to know you as His adopted child? What does it mean to you to be chosen by Him? Does it help you feel accepted? Why or why not?

5. Besides giving you the gift of salvation, how else does your heavenly Father let you know you are highly valued by Him?

6. What statements of truth and verses of Scripture do

you need to repeat to your heart in order to be more open to receiving God's blessings? How can you make them a permanent part of your life?

7. Are there additional Bible verses you can claim in order to triumph over the enemy's lies and destructive thought patterns? What are they? Are you willing to share them with others?

7

BITTERNESS

Freedom from Misery

MANY YEARS AGO A WOMAN came to me for pastoral counseling, and from the moment she walked in the door, I could tell she had a very heavy, bitter heart. It was written all over her belligerent and haggard countenance.

I realized immediately she was not there for a pleasant visit, but frankly I was still a bit surprised when she said, "Pastor, I get so irritated every time you talk about God's love. I can't stand that word—*love*. It just doesn't exist, at least not in my world."

"What word does fit your world?" I asked her.

"Hate," she replied painfully. I was stunned. That caught me off guard.

Taking a cue from my silence, she forged ahead and explained, "I grew up in a world of hate—hatred of the neighbors, of other races, of the rich people on the hill, and of everything that my father thought kept us in poverty. I heard a lot about hate when I was a child. And I'm still forced to learn more about it every day."

She continued, "I abhor lots of things about my life. I detest the way my husband treats me, the way my children act, and the way my boss at the mill is so mean and demanding. I can't stand the way I look. I loathe where we live. And I especially despise the doctor who just told me I have cancer."

My heart broke for her. I could not imagine the pain she'd experienced throughout her life—and how difficult it had to be to receive the terrifying diagnosis on top of it all. It was no wonder she did not like associating the word *love* with God. With so much animosity in her life, how could she?

I asked as gently as I could, "What would you like me to do for you?"

"I want you to pray that I get healed," she answered.

The real healing she needed was in her spirit—she needed freedom from her ingrained hatred and bitterness.

So I did. As she sat in my office, I asked the Father to cure her body of the cancer. But even as I interceded for her, I knew that the real healing she needed was in her spirit—she needed freedom from her ingrained hatred and bitterness. As long as her wounded emotions went untreated, she would be miserable—not living the life that God had created her to experience.

TWO TRUTHS

I address the topic of bitterness now—after fear and rejection—because it is important to recognize that as we think about our emotions and how they originate, we will want to assign blame for our woundedness. You can see this clearly in the case of the woman who came to me for prayer. She was taught from early on to despise those who had any part of her misfortune—whether their participation in her adversity was real or imagined. Did her doctor cause her cancer or wish to inflict pain on her by revealing her diagnosis? Of course not. His goal was to help heal her of it. However, because he was the bearer of the bad tidings, she blamed him for her pain.

Likewise, you will be tempted to assign responsibility for the hurt you experience. You may fault others because of the way they treated you and the heartache they caused you. You may condemn yourself for poor choices, past mistakes, or because of an inherent sense of unworthiness. Or you may think that God is to blame for what's happened to you and question why He has allowed such painful circumstances in your life. Regardless of whom you hold accountable for the hurt in your soul, one thing is sure—if you don't let it go, you will continue to experience bondage.

If you don't let it go, you will continue to experience bondage.

Therefore, at the outset of dealing with bitterness, we must recognize two truths:

1. Denying That Your Bitterness Exists Doesn't Work—So Acknowledge It

God understands how destructive bitterness is to our souls. He knows that when we are filled with hate or trapped in unforgiveness, we are severely hurting ourselves. This is why the Lord wants us to trust Him to help us forgive and admonishes us, "Let all bitterness and wrath and anger and clamor and slander be put away from you, along with all malice. Be kind to one another, tender-hearted, forgiving each other, just as God in Christ also has forgiven you" (Eph. 4:31–32).

Unfortunately, our tendency is often to deny our resentment and animosity instead of actually dealing with these emotions and forgiving. We do not like to admit we are plagued with such ugly feelings. So we either try to justify our anger as righteous indignation or we deny that it exists at all.

Therefore, the first truth we must realize is that in order to be free of the damaging emotion of bitterness, we must agree with God that it exists in us.

Sadly, refusing to acknowledge we are resentful traps us in bondage. Instead of confronting the source of our pain and confessing—"Lord, I concede there is bitterness in me; please help me to overcome it"—we prefer to pretend it's not there. We ignore it—allowing the buried acid of bitterness to wreak havoc on our hearts. This brings us to point number two.

2. Bitterness Continues to Wound as Long as It Persists—So Root It Out

The second thing we must understand is that whether we refuse to confront our bitterness or purposely hold on to it, that bitterness continues to wound us and keep us in bondage as long as it exists.

One of the most dangerous things we can ever do is underestimate how destructive bitterness is. Resentment doesn't just "go away," diminishing over time. We may forget the events that caused the devastating emotions, but our bodies continue to bear the effects of them. Rather, we must actively rid animosity from our lives in order to be truly free of it.

This is why we are taught in Hebrews 12:15, "See to it that no one comes short of the grace of God; that no root of bitterness springing up causes trouble, and by it many be defiled." We may think that by suppressing or internalizing our anger, we are maintaining control. But make no mistake about it—our resentment continues to be a force for destruction as long as it is present in us.

I saw this truth firsthand in the life of a member of our fellowship. It was many years ago, and I recall this man was very committed to God. He taught Sunday school and was a fine example to everyone he instructed. Sadly, when sickness befell his three-year-old son and the little boy died, all that changed. The man became angry toward the Lord, the church, and anyone who crossed his path.

It's understandable that this fellow would have a lot to wrestle with—who could bear the loss of a beloved child? Unfortunately, he did not understand how to deal with the feelings of pain and bereavement that he was experiencing, or how dangerous it was for him to hold on to them. So he went into an absolute tailspin and his emotions took control in a devastating manner. Bitterness festered within him until his life was characterized with hostility and resentment.

This believer lost far more than his boy—he forfeited his life, health, effectiveness for the kingdom of God, and relationships as well.

This is an example of why it is imperative that we guard our hearts and make sure that bitterness does not take root in us. Although anger is a natural emotion for us to feel—especially in times of great loss and injury—it is extremely destructive when we hold on to and nurture it. If we neither acknowledge our resentment nor deal with it in a godly manner, it can do us and our loved ones even greater harm.

> *It is imperative that we guard our hearts and make sure that bitterness does not take root in us.*

WHAT BITTERNESS AND UNFORGIVENESS PRODUCE SPIRITUALLY

The practical consequences of unforgiveness and bitterness, of course, are numerous and disastrous—affecting our health, spiritual lives, and relationships. This is why you and I need to ensure that we deal with them if we see them becoming evident in our lives. And let me assure you, resentment *will* become apparent if it resides within you. Few things in life are more destructive to our lives, conduct, conversation, and character than a lack of forgiveness—and nothing is more difficult to hide.

Of course, bitterness impacts our health and relationships similarly to the ways fear and rejection do—so we will not repeat those discussions here. What we will examine is how resentment affects us spiritually. At times we realize that something is hindering our relationship with God, but we cannot pinpoint what it is. We try to grow in our intimacy with the Lord, but are unable to make any strides. This may very well be due to a desire to blame others and a spirit of unforgiveness that desperately need to be rooted out.

1. Bitterness Hinders Our Prayer Life

First, Jesus made it very clear that if we insist on harboring animosity—refusing to let go of the wounds we've received from others—we cannot be right with Him. He warned, "If you do not forgive others, then your Father will not forgive your transgressions" (Matt. 6:15).

This doesn't mean you will lose your salvation. Rather, it indicates that every time you go before the throne of grace and the Lord sees a bitter spirit, He will insist that you deal with your unwillingness to pardon others. Eventually, you must either agree with Him or it will hinder your intimacy with Him.

Make no mistake, unwillingness to forgive is a very serious thing—completely counter to what God teaches us and how He hopes to work through us in the world (2 Tim. 2:24–26). We simply cannot maintain a bitter heart and still enjoy an effective prayer life (Matt. 5: 38–43).

2. Bitterness Impedes Our Worship

A second problem that arises is our inability to truly worship the Lord properly when bitterness inhibits our praises. After all, what is worship? I believe it has three distinct aspects:

- Worship includes an overflowing sense of *awe and adoration* toward the Lord.
- We pour out our hearts to Him in *joy and thanksgiving* and express how grateful we are to Him.
- And we completely *focus on Him*—not on our own needs, hurts, or offenses—just on His awesome, unfailing, perfect, and matchless character.

But when we are bitter, we cannot do any of that. Why? Because first, how can we truly adore and praise the God who let that terrible thing happen to us? In our hearts, we always harbor some doubt of His motives. *After all,* we think, *He is sovereign God—why did He allow that pain into our lives?*

If we refuse to believe anything beneficial can come from our adverse circumstances, we will not find it possible to be grateful.

Second, we will most likely be unable to thank Him when we are angry that He allowed that adversity to reach us. First Thessalonians 5:18 teaches us, "In everything give thanks; for this is God's will for you in Christ Jesus," but that is very difficult to practice if we do not first trust the promise of Romans 8:28: "We know that God causes all things to work together for good to those who love God, to those who are called according to His purpose." If we refuse to believe anything beneficial can come from our adverse circumstances, we will not find it possible to be grateful.

And third, our worship is impeded because we're not truly focused on Him, rather, we are occupied—at least in part—with the pain we feel. You see, God is clear—we are instructed to honor Him by pardoning others (Eph. 4:32). Therefore, whenever we choose to disobey His command, we are actually making that pain more important to our lives than He is. We will either obey Him as sovereign almighty God and forgive those who hurt us or we will hold on to our right to be offended and make it an idol in our lives (1 John 4:19–21).

3. Bitterness Prevents Peace in a Church Body

Like many pastors, I began my work in a very small church— Fruitland Baptist near Hendersonville, in the mountains of North Carolina. This was a wonderful group of people, and I grew to love them very much. But as is true of many small congregations, this church had a number of families who were embroiled in some terrible conflicts. None of the quarrels were as bad as the infamous feud between the Hatfields and the McCoys, thankfully, but there were quite a few hindering the genuine love that should characterize a church.

At one point, I discovered that two families had been engaged in an especially heated argument for years, but I could not pinpoint the origin of the dispute. So I asked both families, separately, what had caused them to develop such animosity. Neither could tell me the source of their hostility toward each other. The antagonism had simply festered until it characterized their every interaction.

No church can sustain harmony and a focus on the Great Commission (Matt. 28:19–20) under such circumstances. How right David was when he said, "How good and how pleasant it is for brothers to dwell together in unity!" (Ps. 133:1). But when bitterness takes root, the peace in the church suffers.

4. Bitterness Damages a Person's Ability to Represent Christ

Can you imagine how horrible it would have been if God had stopped at a particular sin in your life and said, "No, this one isn't pardoned because it's just too terrible. There is no possible way I could ever forgive you of *that*." It would be heartbreaking, because that one transgression would keep you separated from your loving heavenly Father forever (James 2:10).

Thankfully, the Lord would never do that to us—He wouldn't pick and choose which sins to forgive once we've repented. Because at the cross, Jesus forgave all our iniquity—past, present, and future—and once we accept Him as Savior, every single transgression is pardoned without exception (Acts 10:42–43; 1 John 1:9).

However, that's exactly what we do when we refuse to forgive others of what they've done to us—we choose which sins are pardonable and which are not. Instead of releasing them completely as Jesus did for us, we choose to hold on to our hurt, resentment, and hostility. We want to keep punishing them in our hearts.

And that is precisely what bitterness is—*refusing to give others what God has freely given to us.* We decline to give up our resentment toward them and cling to a "right" to get even that can't be found anywhere in God's Word. This, in turn, hurts our relationship with the Father, impedes our spiritual growth, and stops us from testifying of His grace to others. Think about it: How can we represent Jesus to a lost and dying world when we refuse to act like Him—forgiving freely? It is simply not possible.

> How can we represent Jesus to a lost and dying world when we refuse to act like Him—forgiving freely? It is simply not possible.

Throughout my years in ministry, I have witnessed a number of husbands and wives who were seemingly unable to resolve conflicts with each other or to pardon past hurts. The more the parents squabbled, the more unruly their children became—fighting at school and showing disrespect to authority figures. School counselors often call this "acting out," but more than likely, they are simply imitating Mom and Dad. When a child grows up in a negative home full of contention and strife, it is difficult for that child to develop healthy and godly relationships with their peers because it is not modeled to them effectively. They will mimic what they see and hear.

Likewise, when we allow bitterness and unforgiveness to drive us, it clouds our thinking, goads our actions, blocks the Holy Spirit's activity in us, and blinds us to God's purposes. We simply cannot be good examples to those who need Jesus or effectively exhibit His character of love, joy, peace, patience, kindness, goodness, faithfulness, gentleness, and self-control (Gal. 5:22–23).

In fact, quite the opposite becomes true about us. Asaph affirms in Psalm 73:21–22 (NLT), "I realized that my heart was bitter, and I was all torn up inside. I was so foolish and ignorant—I must have seemed like a senseless animal." In other words, instead of exhibiting Christ's holy, loving, and wise character, we are out of control—reactive, hostile, and irrational. This is because when we allow bitterness to reside in us, it slowly takes over and drives us. It prevents us from allowing the Lord to lead and work in us; therefore, we no longer have self-control, which is a fruit of the Spirit (Gal. 5:23).

What type of witness does that produce? What Christ-like character can we demonstrate to others? Jesus was clear: "By this all men will know that you are My disciples, if you have love for one another" (John 13:35). But when resentment characterizes our lives, we cannot be loving witnesses to others or grow spiritually.

REASONS PEOPLE CHOOSE NOT TO FORGIVE OTHERS

Scripture is clear: "The churning of anger produces strife" (Prov. 30:33). You cannot live a happy, healthy, effective, fruitful life if you are harboring unresolved resentment. And God can free you from the bondage to bitterness if you will allow Him to purify your heart and instruct you. But if forgiving others is so important, and the consequences for refusing to do so are so great, then why are people so reluctant to let go of their animosity?

Ultimately, unforgiveness is really the need to create a sense of control in the situation—to direct our own destiny and feel secure. For example, the person wronged may wish to ensure the offender's punishment. So he may say, "If I forget the evil done to me, the offender will go scot-free and what she did will be forgotten." In essence, the individual believes his resentment and bitterness somehow holds the other person accountable for what she has done—as if it is his responsibility to ensure the wrongdoer doesn't get away with it. Of course, we know that the only rightful judge is God Himself—and He knows exactly how to exact justice and set the offender on the right path. This is why Paul admonished, "Never take your own revenge, beloved, but leave room for the wrath of God, for it is written, 'VENGEANCE IS MINE, I WILL REPAY,' says the Lord" (Rom. 12:19).

> *Ultimately, unforgiveness is really the need to create a sense of control in the situation.*

A second reason people give for not letting go of their bitterness is that they blame themselves for what happened—whether they were at fault or not. Often this is because of the fear of rejection or a pervasive feeling of guilt. Additionally, they may be frightened by their anger or may feel it is an inappropriate response, so they deny it exists and inadvertently turn it inward. Because of this, they may be tempted to heap additional condemnation upon themselves by saying such things as, "I was so gullible." "I should have known better." Or, "I allowed myself to be influenced by people I never should have trusted." We will cover this more in depth in Chapter 8 when we examine guilt; however, we should note that this is a very real, destructive, and dysfunctional way to create a false feeling of security when adversity occurs.

A third way a person may try to establish a sense of control over their circumstances is to assert that she has a "right" to her bitterness—especially when she is haunted by an experience for a long time. In order to validate how profoundly the offense affected her, she may feel it necessary to repeatedly bring the wrong done to her to the surface—reminding others of what is to blame for her condition. She may explain, "I don't think I'll ever be able to forget what happened or how much it hurt me." Ultimately, however, what she is doing is hiding in her pain and avoiding the fear involved when moving forward.

At one point or another, we all want to protect ourselves and blame others when terrible things occur. Since the Garden of Eden, this has been an integral part of our fallen nature (Gen. 3:11–13). The question, then, is, Are you denying your need to forgive, and if so, why? Are you trying to restore feelings of authority and security by holding on to your bitterness? Are you trying to punish someone for how he or she hurt you?

Friend, stop deceiving yourself—you are not hurting the person who wounded you. You're only trapping yourself in a prison of misery. You can become so afraid of being hurt again that you isolate yourself and shut yourself off from receiving the love you so desperately need. Do not forfeit the peace and joy that should rightfully be yours as a child of God by allowing memories of that person's actions to repeatedly torment you. Doing so will cost you your health, emotional stability, and relationships with the people who love you.

It is understandable that you're angry and afraid of letting go of what has been done. You don't want to ever be in that situation again, and you don't want anyone else to be either. But what you must understand is that *forgiveness doesn't mean you deny that what happened was wrong, and it certainly doesn't mean you allow that person to abuse you again.*

> *Forgiveness doesn't mean you deny that what happened was wrong, and it certainly doesn't mean you allow that person to abuse you again.*

You can stop the wound that person has inflicted from hurting you. As a child of God, you have the freedom and the ability to walk away from such a hurtful situation through forgiveness. So give the situation to the Father. Release the offender to the Lord and step out of the bondage. Make the choice to forgive them, so God can begin freeing you of the terrible consequences of bitterness. He can heal you and help you to set up strong, healthy boundaries in your life that will restore your confidence and your sense of well-being.

GAINING VICTORY OVER UNFORGIVENESS

The truth of the matter is, God has not only given you the mandate to forgive (Eph. 4:32) but He has also empowered you with the ability to release the wrongs done to you—no matter how deeply they affect your soul or have become part of your identity. Your heavenly Father desires to restore you.

I know it is true because I have seen the wonderful release of forgiveness firsthand. When I was nine years old, my mother remarried because she believed that I needed a father. Unfortunately, as I said in the previous chapter, my stepfather, John, turned out to be a very bitter, abrasive man who never showed us any kindness, love, or affection. As a child growing up in that hostile environment, I developed quite a spirit of unforgiveness toward him.

As the years went by, I grew up, went to college, and eventually began pastoring my first church. You might think that I'd forgotten John's cruelty or that somehow it no longer mattered. But it did—deeply. So the Lord began convicting me of my need to not only pardon John but also to ask him for forgiveness because of my attitude. So I made arrangements to go see him.

I remember how he and I sat across the table from each other that evening. It was difficult, but I said to him, "John, the reason I came home was to ask you to forgive me for my unforgiving spirit toward you." When I finished speaking, John started to weep—big tears running down his face. Then my stepfather—the man who'd never shown me any affection whatsoever—got up, came around the table, hugged me tightly, and asked me to forgive him for the way he had treated my mother and me. It was an incredibly freeing night for both of us.

It was an incredibly freeing night for both of us.

God can liberate you of this terrible emotion as well. Don't continue in it for another minute. In prayer, give whatever wounded you to Him and express your trust in Him to heal you. How do you do so?

1. Ask God to Reveal Any Bitterness in You

Unforgiveness is serious business. As you pray, consider these questions: Are you caustic, critical, overly suspicious of others, or easily offended? Do you lash out unexpectedly? Do certain subjects set you off? Is something hindering your relationship with God? These are evidences that bitterness has taken hold in your heart. When others touch anywhere near the open wound of resentment in you, a wave of anger, grief, or fear may engulf you.

This is because when we act out of our damaged emotions, we do not respond rationally or in a manner that coincides with the principles of Scripture; rather, we simply react. We are so driven by our woundedness—or the desire to protect ourselves against more pain—that we respond automatically in a negative and destructive way.

In fact, even thinking about this subject may be extremely painful for you because bitterness burns deep into your heart like acid. But as long as you deny that the emotions exist, you are merely repressing them. They continue to control you. Therefore, listen to the Lord and acknowledge any resentment He reveals in you—even if it is from an event or situation you thought you had already forgiven. In doing so, you take an important step toward taking hold of the peace He desires for you to enjoy.

2. Assume Full Responsibility and Ask God for Forgiveness

As the Father reveals areas of bitterness, agree with Him that you have sinned by harboring unforgiveness. Accept what He says fully—He is God and you are not. He can see where there is bondage in your soul, and His goal is to free you from it.

It may be painful. You will probably want to fight it. The feelings that rise up in your heart may be agonizing and confusing. And it is likely you will be tempted to say, "Wait, this is just not fair. That person should be asking *me* for forgiveness. Why should I have to confess? I've not hurt them in any way." But even this reveals that you are harboring destructive anger and you must accept responsibility for your unforgiving spirit.

This part of the process is not about how you responded to the offender, but what the Lord sees in your heart—what is hindering your relationship with Him. Recall what King David wrote in Psalm 51: "Against You, You only, I have sinned and done what is evil in Your sight, so that You are justified when You speak and blameless when You judge. . . . Behold, You desire truth in the innermost being, and in the hidden part You will make me know wisdom" (vv. 4, 6).

> *This part of the process is not about how you responded to the offender, but what the Lord sees in your heart—what is hindering your relationship with Him.*

God is acutely aware of what is going on inside of you in ways you could never imagine. Therefore, trust

Him to know how to free you. If He reveals something as a barrier to intimacy, ask the Father to forgive you of it and of any way you've resisted His work in your life. Then commit your hope and future to Him anew.

3. Ask God to Help You Forgive the Offender

Once you experience the Father's forgiveness, hopefully it will be easier to put yourself in the shoes of those who have wronged you and to understand things from their perspective. After all, we are all sinful and in need of grace. Just as woundedness, bondage, and the sin within you have at times prompted you to behave hurtfully, you can imagine how the pain of past injuries may have driven the offender to lash out at you (Matt. 18:21–35).

This is exactly how the Lord increased my love for my stepfather and showed me how to give up my right to retaliate against him: He gave me insight into the pain that caused John to react so negatively. The Father also helped me see that John was not my enemy—sin, unforgiveness, and bitterness were. I realized that to pardon what he had done was to show the sacrificial, unconditional love of Christ in a real and tangible way.

I can still remember going to see my stepfather and afterward thinking, *Father, how grateful I am that I now have good feelings toward John. I praise You for helping me understand John better and for showing me that the source of his bitterness and resentment is that his father refused to let him go to college to become a doctor. Knowing the source of his woundedness has grown my compassion and love for him.*

The Lord helped me overcome my painful feelings toward John, and He can do so for you as well. That does not make a past offense right, and it doesn't necessarily mean the offender will stop trying to hurt you, but God will lead you to peace in the situation. The Father will also increase your understanding of His awesome love for you and how you can show it to others. As Paul says, "Perhaps God will change those people's hearts, and they will learn the truth. Then they will come to their senses and escape from the devil's trap" (2 Tim. 2:25–26, NLT).

For this reason, do not by any means respond to God's promptings with, "That situation doesn't really affect me anymore, Lord. Whenever it comes up, I just push it to the back of my mind and ignore it. I've already forgiven that person. Really, I'm ok." No, you are not. He is bringing it up for a purpose— to liberate you and heal your brokenness *thoroughly*. Therefore, ask Him to give you more understanding on how you can forgive completely.

Ask Him to give you more understanding on how you can forgive completely.

Now, whether a full pardon must involve a face-to-face meeting is between you and the Father—you will need to ask the Lord to reveal if it is necessary. The truth of the matter is there are times when it is either necessary or simply better for you to release your bitterness toward a person in the presence of God alone, without ever confronting him or her about what was done. However, more often than not, it is constructive to go and talk to the individual about what has occurred in order to heal the relationship. I believe God will answer your sincere request for His guidance.

If the person who has hurt you has died, then of course a conversation with him or her will not be possible. However, I have found through the years that many people benefit from an exercise that I call "the empty chair." What you can do is sit opposite an empty chair and imagine that the person is seated across from you. Confess your resentment of what that individual has done. Do not use this time to blame the other person or to air all of your grievances—that is neither helpful nor necessary. Rather, admit that you felt wounded by his or her actions and that you had difficulty letting it go. Then, ask the other person to forgive you and express your sincere desire to be reconciled to him or her.

This is a one-way conversation, of course, but if you do this with a humble heart—asking God to help you voice all that needs to be said and to be open to the Holy Spirit—you will be amazed at how He takes care of the rest.

4. Pray, with Thanksgiving, for the Person Who Wounded You

Jesus said it Himself: "Love your enemies and pray for those who persecute you, so that you may be sons of your Father who is in heaven" (Matt. 5:44–45). Why did He do so? Again, this is so He can continue to heal your wound, transform your heart, and give you His perspective about the situation.

Remember, 1 John 4:19–21 admonishes, "We love, because He first loved us. If someone says, 'I love God,' and hates his brother, he is a liar; for the one who does not love his brother whom he has seen, cannot love God whom he has not seen. And this commandment we have from Him, that the one who loves God should love his brother also." In other words, every person and trial the Lord allows into your life—including the one you're struggling with right now—presents an opportunity for Him to demonstrate His love, character, and faithfulness to you and to others through your testimony. If you hate someone because of what the Father is trying to teach you through him, then, in reality, you despise God and the purpose He has for your life.

But if you can look at the adversity as an opportunity to exhibit your faith and show His love to others, then you will grow in Christ's character and likeness. Romans 8:34 teaches us, "Jesus is He who died, yes, rather who was raised, who is at the right hand of God, who also intercedes for us." Likewise, Hebrews 7:25 reminds us, "He always lives to make intercession" for us. When you pray for those you have pardoned—you are imitating the Savior, doing just as He does for you.

> *If you can look at the adversity as an opportunity to exhibit your faith and show His love to others, then you will grow in Christ's character and likeness.*

Likewise, you can gratefully give thanks to the Father, because you know He is working through whatever wounded you in order to give you insight into human nature, bring you closer into fellowship with Him, and mold you into a vessel worthy of His use. The apostle Peter affirms, "Don't be surprised at the fiery trials you are going through, as if something strange were happening to you. Instead, be very glad—for these trials make you partners with Christ in His suffering, so that you will have the wonderful joy of seeing his glory when it is revealed to all the world" (1 Pet. 4:12–13, NLT). He is using this trial for your good; therefore, give Him thanks (Rom. 8:28).

CONTINUE TO PURSUE FULL FORGIVENESS

So how do you know when you have fully forgiven others? You simply won't see the people who hurt you in the same way. The harsh feelings that you had toward them will be replaced by a new love and understanding. You will want them to experience the Lord's deep tenderness, healing, and grace. And you will find that you have a new ability to accept people just as they are—realizing that God is not finished with them yet, but that they have potential to love and serve Him as well. You look forward to the day when they become all that the Father created them to be.

What this all means in practical terms is that you will also have a different response to them when you encounter them in public.

Shortly after I came to Atlanta, I developed a friendship with a man whom I loved deeply as a brother in Christ. I was very grateful for his camaraderie and partnership in the gospel and said so often. And I really thought he loved and supported me, too. But the truth is, he didn't. He simply pretended to be my friend in order to achieve his own goals—undermining my authority as pastor of First Baptist Atlanta and trying to get rid of me. Thankfully, the Lord spared me from what the man wanted to accomplish. But I was absolutely devastated when I discovered that he had purposely planned to harm me and that he had no remorse over what he had done.

I struggled with being merciful and forbearing toward him, but not for long. I was well aware that if I didn't let all of my anger and resentment go, I would suffer from bitterness and unforgiveness. So I forgave him completely and asked God to help me be gracious to him, should I ever see him again.

Then one day I was attending a session of the Southern Baptist Convention and I saw this man walking across the large rotunda. He was headed in my direction, but he was talking with someone and didn't see me in his path. Suddenly I was acutely aware that the Father had answered my prayers for healing and forgiveness. Instead of any discomfort in seeing him, I had a wonderful spirit of total freedom. I couldn't wait for him to get closer so I could greet him warmly, ask about his family and work, and invite him to worship at First Baptist.

Of course, he seemed to express some awkwardness when he realized I was standing in his path and that he couldn't sidestep me. But as I welcomed him with a smile and extended my hand to shake his, his countenance relaxed and we were able to chat in an amicable manner. The bitterness was gone and friendly feelings were revived. And quite frankly, I believe many wounds were healed and God was glorified through that encounter.

Friend, I know you have most likely faced a great deal. It is easy to blame and difficult to forgive. However, I admonish you for the sake of your future, let go of the bitterness and allow God to heal you. Stop living with the misery caused by acid unforgiveness. Choose today to pardon those who have wronged you.

It won't be easy and you will most likely have to go to the throne of grace often for help and guidance (Heb. 4:14–16). But if you will let go of the blame, God *will* heal, comfort, and protect you. He will also free you from your bondage and make you an example of His restoration and a vessel of His love (2 Cor. 1:3–7).

Therefore, allow the Father to have His way in your heart. He will certainly make sure that no tear you ever shed, no pain you ever feel, and no tragedy you ever experience will go without notice or without the promise of redemption.

Father, I come before You today, broken—asking for the very thing I was not strong enough to give—grace. I know unforgiveness is a serious offense in Your eyes, and I accept full responsibility for my bitter spirit. But please forgive me, Father, and help me to lay down blame for my wounds so I will not have to lose another night's sleep over it. Send Your Holy Spirit to teach me how to forever cast aside my bondage to bitterness and resentment so I can be healed. And please restore what has been lost through my stubbornness.

Lord, I pray for the people who have hurt me and ask You to please help me understand what motivated them to do so. Show me their hearts, Father—what pain, confusion, and bondage lies deep within, so I may feel mercy for them. Help me have compassion on their situation, and show me how to demonstrate Your love and grace to them in an active and tangible way.

Father, I am so grateful for Your promise to pick me up even when I stumble and fall. Thank You for showing me how to be free of unforgiveness and live a life worthy of Your name. Truly, there is none more merciful, compassionate, loving, and kind than You. In Jesus' name I pray. Amen.

QUESTIONS FOR
PERSONAL REFLECTION AND GROUP STUDY

1. Can you think of situations or people that you have blamed for your wounded spirit? Ask God to reveal them to you and make a list. Then ask Him to help you forgive each one.

2. Have you ever seen bitterness take hold of and eventually ruin a person's life to the point of total ineffectiveness, spiritually and relationally? What happened?

3. Have you noticed times when resentful feelings have affected your prayer life and worship? What changes did you need to make in order to get back on track with God?

4. Have you ever seen bitterness toward others keep you

from having a healthy emotional life? How did these feelings affect you?

5. When is the last time you accepted the full responsibility of your unforgiving spirit and handed it over to God to help you deal with it effectively?

6. How do people act when they feel it is their right to pay back wrongdoing to other people who have hurt them? Have you ever acted that way? How did that work out for you?

7. How has God spoken to you about the root of bitterness and the inability to forgive others through this chapter? What steps are you going to take to get beyond this issue of resentment?

8

GUILT

Relief from the Ultimate Weight on Your Soul

SUPPOSE YOU GREW UP IN a home where no matter what you did or how well you performed, you were never really sure you had your father's approval. You tried as hard as you could, of course, and did everything he asked you to do to the best of your ability. But he never responded to you in a meaningful way—at least, none you could perceive. So you always felt an ominous cloud of uncertainty hanging over you because you were never quite sure of where you stood with Him. Consequently, you frequently wondered, "Is my father pleased with me? What does that look on his face mean? Have I done something to offend him? Why won't he speak to me?"

Naturally, this would affect you tremendously as you grew up, putting you in bondage to insecurity, inadequacy, and doubt. It would be absolutely impossible to develop any kind of closeness with him or to trust him to any degree. You would always be left wondering if your father really accepted you and if you were worthy of his love.

Sadly, this is the way many people live the Christian life. They live with a continuous fear that they have invoked God's divine displeasure and never truly know His joy, comfort, and loving care. They do not experience the beautiful feeling of being safely wrapped in His omnipotent arms and sheltered with His awesome salvation.

Have you experienced the beautiful feeling of being safely wrapped in His omnipotent arms and sheltered with His awesome salvation?

Instead, they continually ask, "Am I pleasing the Father? I always feel so guilty—I must have done something wrong. He is probably angry at me—why else would He continue to send all of these trials and difficulties?" They perceive Him to be a God of wrath and punishment, rather than the loving Savior who willingly gave up all things so we could be permanently reconciled to Him (Phil. 2:5–11).

Now you and I know that God is holy and just and will always judge sin. But we should also recognize that He is caring, kind, and good. It is not His desire to castigate us. In fact, even when we need correction, as the nation of Judah did during the time of the Babylonian captivity, we must count on the fact that "The Lord will not reject forever, for if He causes grief, then He will have compassion according to His abundant lovingkindness. For He does not afflict willingly or grieve the sons of men" (Lam. 3:31–33). Likewise, 2 Peter 3:9 reminds us, "The Lord is . . . patient toward you, not wishing for any to perish but for all to come to repentance."

In other words, the Father's goal is for us to have a loving, intimate relationship with Him. Yes, difficult things may happen in our lives, but they are not for our punishment—they are to help us grow, teach us to cling to Him more closely, and to cleanse us from the bondage to sin (Zech. 13:9).

So if God is gracious and tender-hearted toward us, then why do feelings of guilt continue to plague so many believers? From where do the feelings of condemnation originate, if not from the Father?

The Father's goal is for us to have a loving, intimate relationship with Him.

This is why it is now time to turn our attention to a topic that at times holds the key to a great deal of our suffering: *how we feel about ourselves.*

In this world, there is most likely no one who is as critical of you as you are. In fact, you have the potential to pick yourself apart with greater intensity and cruelty than anyone else ever could or would think to. No one else can torment you with negative thoughts every waking minute as you can.

Perhaps you are like so many other people who rehash their failures and feelings of worthlessness—totally missing the joy and abundant life God has for them. It is also possible that you fear the Lord's punishment—you are positive He is just waiting to catch you messing up in order to discipline you. Or maybe you have come to believe that you are inherently damaged and will never experience real love because you've made far too many mistakes. You simply cannot forgive yourself for who you are and what you have done. And you can easily trace the roots of your fear, rejection, and bitterness to the condemnation you feel toward yourself.

Does this sound about right? Do you harbor unforgiveness toward yourself? Do you beat yourself up because of the emptiness you feel, because of unmet expectations, or because of how important relationships have failed? The source of this pain is the enemy of your soul, who Revelation 12:10 calls "the accuser of our brethren." He intensifies the painful wounds within you to keep you distracted from your real purpose, which is to love and serve God.

First Peter 5:8 reminds us, "Be on the alert. Your adversary, the devil, prowls around like a roaring lion, seeking someone to devour." And one of the most effective ways he keeps you from becoming a powerful champion for the kingdom of God is to turn you against yourself—discouraging and paralyzing you from moving forward.

> *One of the most effective ways the enemy keeps you from becoming a powerful champion for the kingdom of God is to turn you against yourself.*

However, let me be very clear: *Just as you don't have a right to keep grudges toward others, you certainly shouldn't tear yourself apart or permit yourself to act in a self-destructive manner.* Romans 8:1 asserts, "There is now no condemnation for those who are in Christ Jesus." If Jesus Christ is your Lord and Savior, you are a child of the living God—forgiven *eternally* and loved *unconditionally.* Yes, you've made mistakes and have sinned against the Father—all of us have (Rom. 3:23). But Jesus understands your weaknesses and has mercy for you because He was "made like His brethren in all things, so that He might become a merciful and faithful high priest in things pertaining to God . . . For since He Himself was tempted in that which He has suffered, He is able to come to the aid of those who are tempted" (Heb. 2:17–18).

He knows the pain, insecurities, and fears you face, and He wants to help you break free from them and from the unforgiveness you feel toward yourself. You don't have to live under a terrible cloud of shame that suffocates your soul.

THE SOURCE OF OUR GUILT

Of course, the first thing we must do to break free from guilt—as is true for every other emotion—is to understand where it originates.

Everyone experiences feelings of self-reproach and remorse at one point or another, and much of it is indeed valid. Before we know Jesus as our Savior, we are judged *legally* culpable—we are pronounced guilty of breaking God's holy Law because of our sin. As James 2:10 reminds us, "Whoever keeps the whole law and yet stumbles in one point, he has become guilty of all."

When we accept Christ as our Savior, we are no longer blameworthy in the legal sense because He pays the full penalty for our sin (Rom. 6:23). However, when we violate God's Word, the Holy Spirit still bears witness of it within us—creating the *emotional* condition of guilt in order to confront the issues He wants us to deal with. The apostle John explains, "The Helper . . . will convict the world concerning sin and righteousness and judgment. . . . When He, the Spirit of truth, comes, He will guide you into all the truth" (John 16:7–8, 13).

In other words, God keeps us in the center of His will through the promptings of the Spirit. When we begin to deviate from His path for us, He convicts us so we will not miss His wonderful purposes for our lives. Those feelings of guilt are our cue to repent and turn back to the Lord.

This is what I like to refer to as *good guilt* because it's His way of warning us that we have strayed into dangerous territory and need to return to Him immediately.

> *When we begin to deviate from His path for us, the Holy Spirit convicts us so we will not miss His wonderful purposes for our lives.*

However, when a person cannot identify a specific reason for why he or she feels blame, there is a big problem. A general sense of condemnation usually does not originate from God. He is typically very specific about how we have violated His will because His desire is for us to completely cease from a particular behavior and walk in the way He commands us to.

Paul explained, "The sorrow that is according to the will of God produces a repentance without regret, leading to salvation, but the sorrow of the world produces death" (2 Cor. 7:10). In other words, the conviction we receive from the Lord leads to our freedom. But the indiscriminate feelings of judgment we feel—that tend to originate from our false beliefs about God or ourselves—result in devastation because they continually bombard, imprison, and depress us.

This is the same principle we saw in Chapter 6 about rejection. The messages that remind us of our wonderful relationship with our heavenly Father bring us life and liberty. But the lies that keep us focused on the sin nature and in a constant state of self-condemnation speed us along the path to destruction (Ps. 16:25). Therefore we must understand that Jesus is not in the business of making us feel guilty; rather, He is working to clean up our lives so we will not wrestle with shame and unworthiness.

So in summary, we must understand these two things:

1. Legitimate Guilt Comes from Violating God's Standard

We experience the internal pressure of conviction when we disobey the Lord and experience His warning to repent and return to the center of His will. Ignoring these feelings and continuing in sin will result in severe consequences.

You could think of this type of guilt as God's red light in your life. It would be wonderful if we could speed through our days with only green traffic lights—with every system set to "Go!" and nothing impeding our progress. We know, however, that red lights exist for our safety and benefit—as well as for the protection of those around us. They warn us of danger. The same is true for both God's commands and the internal witness of His Holy Spirit.

The apostle Paul explains, "All things are lawful for me, but not all things are

The Father is looking out for you and wants to protect you from the destructive consequences, suffering, and hardships that always follow disobedience.

profitable. All things are lawful for me, but I will not be mastered by anything" (1 Cor. 6:12). The Father is looking out for you and wants to protect you from the destructive consequences, suffering, and hardships that always follow disobedience.

Therefore, if there is sin in your life that the Holy Spirit is convicting you of, do not wait any longer. Confess it to God and allow Him to free you from it. You are promised in 1 John 1:9: "If we confess our sins, He is faithful and righteous to forgive us our sins and to cleanse us from all unrighteousness." He will not turn you away. Rather, He has allowed that feeling of guilt so you will seek Him. You can always be certain that your heavenly Father is more than willing to remove anything that stands in the way of your relationship with Him.

But you may be thinking there are many more than just a couple of transgressions that you feel guilty about; rather, perhaps there is a pattern of sinfulness that is keeping you in bondage. Maybe you are participating in a particular habit to dull your painful emotions—such as addiction to illicit substances, gambling, sexual sins, excessive spending, gluttony, escapism through technology, or what have you—and you wonder if the Lord could help you with the sickness in your soul. Yes, He can, and He absolutely will. Allow Christ to take control of the behavior, and ask Him to set you free from it. Even now, God will call to your mind the destructive actions that have a stranglehold on your life. Do not ignore Him.

Now, do not be surprised if the first emotion that strikes your heart is fear and the first thought that comes into your mind is, *There is no way out—even God cannot help me overcome this. And honestly, I am not sure I want Him to.* Be assured, this is the enemy trying to stop you from finding freedom. The Lord is your method of escape— your opportunity to rid yourself of the feelings of guilt and shame. Through Him, you can experience true liberty, restoration, and relief.

> *The Lord is your method of escape. . . . Through Him, you can experience true liberty, restoration, and relief.*

Paul affirmed this when he testified, "What a miserable person I am! Who will free me from this life that is dominated by sin and death? Thank God! The answer is in Jesus Christ our Lord." (Rom. 7:24–25, NLT). David understood this truth as well, which is why he said, "Purify me with hyssop, and I shall be clean; wash me, and I shall be whiter than snow. . . . Create in me a clean heart, O God, and renew a steadfast spirit within me" (Ps. 51:7, 10). He knew that turning away from destructive habits would require turning to the Father and focusing on the good things the Lord had for Him to do.

Galatians 5:1 promises, "It was for freedom that Christ set us free; therefore keep standing firm and do not be subject again to a yoke of slavery." So confess your weaknesses, addictions, areas of enslavement, and trust God to teach you how to resist Satan's lure. Don't live with the shame anymore.

2. False Guilt Comes from Wrong Thinking

False guilt occurs when a person feels condemnation but has not actually committed any wrongdoing. This emotion is not grounded in reality, but its effects are just as devastating, and we can encounter the feeling in three ways.

First, we can experience mistaken shame due to believing something is a sin when it isn't. For example, I grew up in a church that had very strict rules. We were taught that women were forbidden to wear slacks or dresses with short sleeves. It was wrong for boys and girls to swim in the same swimming pool. And it was considered sinful to go to a movie—even a clean one. Of course, when I was a young boy, all the films were wholesome.

I recall going to see a musical in 1947 called *I Wonder Who's Kissing Her Now*, about the life of songwriter Joseph Howard. It starred Mark Stevens and June Haver, and included the song "Hello! Ma Baby," which may be familiar to you. I was fifteen at the time, and after hearing so many messages about the evils of watching movies, I was filled with anxiety and shame as I sat in the theater. I wondered if God were going to destroy the cinema house with a bolt of lightning. That, of course, was false guilt.

Thankfully, as I grew up and searched the Word myself, I discovered that many of the things that the church leaders had labeled "sinful" were not actually listed in the Bible. This is why it is so important to be like the believers at Berea, who studied the Word diligently and tested everything they were taught. Acts 17:11 tells us, "They received the word with great eagerness, examining the Scriptures daily to see whether these things were so." Even though it was the apostle Paul preaching to them, they still wanted to know if what they were hearing was true to the Word of God and according to His will. We should do the same. If we don't, we may end up trapped in legalistic beliefs that continually cause us to experience self-condemnation.

Test to make sure what you are hearing is true to the Word of God and according to His will.

Second, we can experience false guilt over sins that have already been pardoned. I meet far too many people who genuinely feel that the Lord is punishing them for something in the past. So I ask them, "Did you ask God to forgive you?"

Usually they will respond, "Well, yes I did. Several times." When I hear this, I realize it is not pardon they struggle with, but self-condemnation. They have not let the sin go, even though the Lord has.

Friend, you only have to turn your iniquity over to the Father once for it to be forgiven. Psalm 103:12 promises, "As far as the east is from the west, so far has He removed our transgressions from us." You may repeatedly recall what you have done, but God does not. In His mind, it is absolutely forgotten. He promises, "I . . . will blot out your sins for my own sake and will never think of them again" (Isa. 43:25, NLT).

A *third reason we may wrestle with false guilt is due to past experiences that may have been beyond our control but that made us feel damaged, cursed, or sinful all the same.* For example, many children who are abused feel a terrible sense of shame, even though there was absolutely nothing they could have done to stop their assailants. They feel a generalized sense of condemnation and unworthiness that does not seem to go away. My heart breaks for them because of what they've endured and the pain and guilt they needlessly tolerate.

Likewise, people who experience tragic accidents, failures, and the unrealistic expectations of others can feel deep shame and carry heavy burdens they were never meant to bear. They may believe God is continually punishing them and that—no matter how many times they confess—they cannot be forgiven.

At times, people can let go of these feelings once they are identified. But sometimes, the pain of false guilt endures because their emotions become a deeply ingrained part of their self-protection and identity. As we go through the rest of this chapter, we'll examine what the lies surrounding false guilt can do to us and how God's truth can give us victory.

But as I mentioned in the last chapter, we should remember that many people turn their bitterness and condemnation inward because they are trying to establish a sense of control in their situation. This may seem a strange way to establish security, but it demonstrates the complexity of the human mind and how we build our defense systems. Subconsciously and irrationally we grasp for whatever stability we can find in reaction to the situation we are obliged to endure.

> *Nothing makes us feel more helpless or fearful than when unpredictable circumstances outside our influence change our lives.*

You see, nothing makes us feel more helpless or fearful than when unpredictable circumstances outside our influence change our lives. We are forced to accept whatever assails us without the option or ability to alter it. So when everything is in turmoil, where can we turn but to the one place we can control—ourselves.

This, in part, is why we all struggle with self-reliance. How many times have you heard yourself or someone else say, "If I want it done right, I have to do it myself." Or, "The only person I can count on is myself." You may even think, *It is all up to me.* Or when something goes badly, you may blame yourself and automatically ask, *What did I do wrong?* We focus on ourselves—on what we did to cause the trial. Even as believers, we must admit, this is a serious temptation.

But people who are exposed to chaotic conditions—especially in early childhood—sometimes develop the debilitating belief that if they are in some way *responsible* for their terrible circumstances, then they can somehow *control* how the trials affect them. So they punish themselves. We see people do this in countless ways— everything from repeatedly listening to demoralizing songs and eating until they feel sick to cutting and anorexia. These destructive behaviors give them relief because they are controlling the level of pain they receive. They believe if they punish themselves, it will somehow lessen the inner turmoil they feel each day.

Does any of this work? Of course it doesn't. But as I said, it is irrational. People create the sense of control in whatever way they can, even if it is destructive.

This, of course, grieves the heart of God, to whom we can always turn when we face adversity (1 Pet. 5:7). After all, bad things happen to all of us. The rain falls on both the good and the wicked alike (Matt. 5:45). And most of the time there is nothing you or I can do to stop it—especially not by turning inward. But this is precisely the reason we are to turn to God. Recall Jesus' powerful words in Matthew 7:24–27:

> "Everyone who hears these words of Mine and acts on them, may be compared to a wise man who built his house on the rock. And the rain fell, and the floods came, and the winds blew and slammed against that house; and yet it did not fall, for it had been founded on the rock.
>
> "Everyone who hears these words of Mine and does not act on them, will be like a foolish man who built his house on the sand. The rain fell, and the floods came, and the winds blew and slammed against that house; and it fell—and great was its fall."

The storms come to both houses. But one is able to stand firm no matter how intensely the tempest blows—and that is the home built on the Word of God. In other words, if you rely solely on yourself, you will have difficulty when the trials come. But if you focus on the Lord, not only will He help you through it all but you are assured that He will cause "all things to work together for good to those who love God, to those who are called according to His purpose" (Rom. 8:28).

THE CONSEQUENCES OF GUILT

So think about how you operate. Do you have a persistent sense that you have done something wrong? Do you ever beat yourself up—blaming yourself for things beyond your control? Do you often wonder if God is punishing you? Do you watch for bad things to happen to you or your loved ones? If so, you may have false guilt buried deep within your heart. Friend, there is nothing healthy about constant self-condemnation. It is the enemy's trap— a terrible tool in his arsenal that he uses to destroy you.

Of course, whether it is good or false guilt you are feeling, you should not hold on to it. The consequences of harboring your feelings of shame are simply far too costly. Therefore, as you review the effects below of ingrained guilt, prayerfully consider whether any of them are evident in your life.

1. Guilt Stops You from Achieving Your Goals

For example, I have a dear friend with a wonderful intuition for business. Sadly, his father always disheartened him by saying, "You'll never amount to anything. You're a lazy good-for-nothing." Consequently, every time he began to make strides toward accomplishing his objectives, he would sabotage himself and disaster would result. He had accepted his father's condemnation, and something inside him would not allow him to succeed. He simply could not break free from this perception of himself.

So consider the following: Do you consistently sabotage yourself—reacting badly in situations that are important to reaching your goals? Do you find yourself coming up short just as you are achieving significant objectives? Are there words from your past that repetitively play in your mind—messages that remind you of failures, faults, and reasons for condemnation? If so, then it is possible you are wrestling with guilt.

2. Self-Reproach Drains Your Energy and Destroys Your Peace

Many people have no inner calm because of their guilt; they feel absolutely tormented and exhausted by their emotions. And it is no wonder—peacefulness and shame were never meant to coexist in our hearts. There is neither rest nor tranquillity in the soul of a person burdened by unbearable feelings of self-condemnation. It is like sandpaper constantly creating agonizing friction within them—pressing them to be better, do more, make restitution for wrongs they never committed, and punish themselves. Often, people who are burdened with shame will work nonstop to overcome those feelings because of the terrible pain they cause. We simply cannot have joy and serenity while guilt plagues us.

So are you consistently afflicted with a lack of peace? Are you weary in your soul—constantly wondering how you can go on? Do you continuously sense uneasiness within you? Then guilt may be destroying your tranquillity.

3. *Guilt Makes You Feel Insecure*

Financially, professionally, and socially, we may be doing well; but it is still possible that something feels wrong within us—as if something disastrous is going to occur. This is because through guilt, the enemy keeps us anxious that we are in danger of the Lord's judgment. His goal is to focus our attention on all the bad things that could happen to us and our loved ones as punishment for our actions. This, of course, keeps us trapped in fear and in a constant state of self-reproach. As a result, we may become so obsessed with the idea we are going to lose our friends and family members that we forget to enjoy them whenever they are around. Additionally, our terrible worry and self-condemnation may actually serve to drive our loved ones away because of how possessive, negative, and fearful we become.

So have you found yourself praying, "God, please forgive me!" over and over, but without a specific sin to confess? Do you continuously worry that something bad will happen and fret over the health and safety of your loved ones? Do the people you care about push you away because of your excessive attention to the details of their lives? This may be evidence that you fear God's judgment because of some ingrained guilt.

4. *Persistent Shame Can Cause Physical and Mental Illness*

Psychiatrists, psychologists, and doctors confirm that many physical problems have a root in strong negative feelings, such as guilt, and Scripture confirms the correlation. In Psalm 38:3–6, David wrote: "There is no health in my bones because of my sin. For my iniquities are gone over my head; as a heavy burden they weigh too much for me. My wounds grow foul and fester because of my folly. I am bent over and greatly bowed down; I go mourning all day long." He made the important connection between our spiritual condition and the physical aspects of our lives. There is no doubt about it; guilt eventually takes a terrible toll on our bodies. Therefore, ask yourself, *Does self-reproach play any part in my physical difficulties?*

5. Self-Condemnation Can Cause Compulsive Behavior

Instead of dealing with shame directly, some people try to compensate for the sin in their lives by exhibiting controlling or compulsive behaviors. For example, they may provide excessive service to the church or community, hoping their good works will soothe their feelings of shame. Likewise, they may keep themselves busy with extreme amounts of cleaning, exercise, or work—trying to meet untenable standards of perfection. As we saw before, this is an attempt to establish control and security. However, these activities prevent the hurting individuals from sitting down quietly before the Lord and receiving His comfort.

So do not be fooled—your good works and attempts to achieve unsustainable standards are not helping you; in fact, they are hurting you and keeping you in a wounded state. Activity is often the enemy's substitute for confession and intimacy with God. If he can trap you in compulsive behaviors, he has won half the battle to damage your effectiveness as a believer.

Therefore consider, do you run from one activity to another with little room for rest? Are you consistently seeking a standard of perfection that is impossible to achieve? Are you uncomfortable with moments of quiet and introspection? If so, consider whether the reason you are struggling is that you are trying to escape feelings of guilt.

6. Guilt Can Make Us Vulnerable to Manipulation

Have you ever noticed that at times people will say, "If you really love me, you will _____," and then proceed to express all of their expectations? They try to make a person feel as if she owes them something and will insist that she prove her love by bending to their will. They do so, of course, in order to get her to do as they please. And they know it will work because the person struggling with guilt often feels responsible for other people's happiness and is therefore easily manipulated.

Does this strategy work on you? Do you often feel as if you owe it to others to prove you really care about them by doing whatever they ask? Even if you meet all their requests—fulfilling whatever they require of you—it will never satisfy them. They will always demand something more of you. Friend, this is a terrible trap. Do not allow others to manipulate you by making you feel guilty.

THE LIES OF THE ENEMY

Did you show any of the evidences of ingrained shame and con-demnation? If so, please understand you are not alone. As we've seen before, one of the ways the enemy keeps us in bondage to our emotions is through the feeling of isolation—the idea that we are the only ones struggling. However, you are not the only person ever to wrestle with guilt or to feel that, in some way, you have been created "less than" everyone else—damaged, useless, and unworthy of love. We all feel that way at one point or another.

I confess that I grew up with a great deal of guilt. This, of course, was due in part to the legalistic rules of the church I was attending. But it was also linked to a deep sense of fail-ure and inadequacy that always haunted me. Because of this, I struggled terribly with perfectionism—I felt I had to be faultless in order to be accepted. Of course, God understood my frailty and limitations—He patiently taught me that all of my inadequacies, faults, and fail-ures were taken care of at the cross. But it took a very long time for me to learn to rest in Jesus' matchless righteousness.

God understands our frailty and limitations— He patiently teaches us that all of our inadequacies, faults, and failures were taken care of at the cross.

In fact, I recall a time early in my ministry when I felt respon-sible to do every job in the church without help. After all, I was getting paid to keep the church running. Additionally, I experi-enced tremendous pressure to succeed brilliantly at every task I was given—whether it was preaching, teaching, or keeping everything in working order. If I was unable to perform to the extreme standards I had set for myself, I felt like a complete and utter failure. This, of course, drove me to try harder and harder until I nearly lost my health. Perhaps you have experienced similar times of demanding too much of yourself as well.

However, please understand, *God will never call you to do anything that He does not first equip you to do.* If the Father gives you an assignment, He expects you to carry it with His strength, according to His wisdom, and in His timing. He will not leave you alone to accomplish it by yourself. Rather, His desire is to help you and reveal Himself to others through you. As He said to the people of Jerusalem after they had returned from the Babylonian captivity and were trying to rebuild the temple, "'Not by might nor by power, but by My Spirit,' says the LORD of hosts" (Zech. 4:6).

God will never call you to do anything that He does not first equip you to do.

Eventually, the Lord made it clear to me that I was to pursue three specific priorities. Number one, I was to deepen my relationship with Him through ongoing prayer and study of His Word. As I often say, our intimacy with God—His first priority for our lives—determines the impact of our lives. If He was going to work through me to lead people into a growing relationship with the Savior, my relationship with Him would have to be the primary focus of my life.

Number two, I was to pay more attention to my own health—

managing my schedule and commitments wisely so that I could maintain my energy and strength. Only by doing that would I be able to keep up with all that He was planning to do through the ministry.

And number three, the Lord showed me the importance of Sunday morning—specifically, of the messages He gave me to preach. These sermons are not only how He works to teach others at First Baptist Atlanta but also what He uses to reach the world through In Touch Ministries—in more than fifty languages, on almost three thousand radio and television stations, in every nation on Earth.

I share all that for this purpose: As long as you remain in your guilt—trying to soothe your conscience by your own means—you will always fall short and feel condemned. But when you trust what God says—when you have faith in His Word and His ability to forgive you—you will find freedom. You will not work or chastise yourself to the point of devastation. Instead, you will experience how truly joyful life can be.

RELEASED FROM GUILT— REJOICING IN CHRIST

Are you willing? Are you ready to be free from the false feelings of condemnation that hold you captive? If so, then you must accept one very important fact: *You can never disappoint God. He loves*

> *You can never disappoint God. He loves and accepts you and always will.*

and accepts you and always will. You must take it to heart that He knows your life from beginning to end—every trial and triumph, every fear and failure, every stumble and every success—and He accepts you *completely.*

Let me warn you—accepting this will probably be difficult. The enemy will most likely continue to bombard you ruthlessly with his lies. He may fill your mind with terrible thoughts such as, *I know Jesus is my Savior, but I feel guilty. I just cannot forgive myself. That mistake will always be with me. Maybe, if I try a little harder, perhaps I can be free of this burden on my soul. No, I will always be a failure. I am damaged and deserve the bad breaks I get. Frankly, I don't know if I can go on. I think the Lord is punishing me. And I deserve it—God couldn't possibly forgive or forget what I have done. He couldn't possibly love me.*

If the enemy has been able to successfully take you captive with guilt, he will most likely keep trying to use it as a tool against you. This is why it is so very important for you to take God at His Word, because freedom from guilt begins with your trust in Christ. Following are three steps to enjoying this freedom:

1. Accept Jesus as Your Savior

The first thing you need to do—if you haven't already—is acknowledge your sins before God and accept Christ's death on the cross and resurrection from the dead as payment for your past, present, and future failures.

2. Identify the Cause of Your Guilt

Do your feelings of guilt originate from unforgiven sin? Then you must repent and make whatever restitution God convicts you to render. You may need to ask someone's forgiveness. Perhaps the Father instructs you to seek help for an addiction or confess your failing to someone who can hold you accountable. Whatever He instructs you to do, do it immediately.

However, it may be difficult to pinpoint where your feelings of condemnation come from. If so, then you must make a conscious decision to accept what the Lord says about you and reject the lies of the enemy. Examine the thoughts that cross your mind and counteract them with Scripture.

3. Rest in Him

The final step is full acceptance that Christ's substitutionary death on the cross was sufficient payment for all your sins. It is time to stop making amends and excuses—you simply cannot serve, come to church, give money, or pray enough to absolve your guilt. You must accept that every sin has been forgiven by the Savior and rest in His awesome provision.

We can find a good illustration of this in history, around the time when the New Testament was written. It was common practice to post a ledger outside a prisoner's cell door declaring his guilt. When he completed his sentence, a certificate was produced, bearing the declaration, "Paid in Full." From that point on, there was absolute proof of the debt's payment. Likewise, Colossians 2:14 (NLT) reports, "He canceled the record of the charges against us and took it away by nailing it to the cross."

Therefore, whenever past sins and failures come to mind and the enemy torments you with thoughts that you are damaged, cursed, or rejected by God, remember that all your failings have been paid in full by the all-sufficient, substitutionary death of Jesus. Say it out loud, "There is absolute proof that this debt has been paid, and I no longer bear it. It has been nailed irrevocably to the cross and forever forgiven in the sight of God. I am free, and I refuse to pick it up again." Then enjoy the freedom that comes from resting fully in Him.

THE ENEMY'S LIE	GOD'S TRUTH— OUR DEFENSE
I know Jesus is my Savior, but I just feel guilty.	There is now no condemnation for those who are in Christ Jesus. —ROMANS 8:1

THE ENEMY'S LIE	GOD'S TRUTH— OUR DEFENSE
I just cannot forgive myself.	You desire truth in the innermost being, and in the hidden part You will make me know wisdom. Purify me with hyssop, and I shall be clean; wash me, and I shall be whiter than snow. —PSALM 51:6–7
That mistake will always be with me.	If anyone is in Christ, he is a new creature; the old things passed away; behold, new things have come. —2 CORINTHIANS 5:17
If I just try a little harder, maybe I can be free of this burden on my soul.	By grace you have been saved through faith; and that not of yourselves, it is the gift of God; not as a result of works, so that no one may boast. —EPHESIANS 2:8–9

THE ENEMY'S LIE	GOD'S TRUTH— OUR DEFENSE
I will always be a failure.	Thanks be to God, who always leads us in triumph in Christ, and manifests through us the sweet aroma of the knowledge of Him in every place. —2 CORINTHIANS 2:14
I am damaged and deserve the bad breaks I get.	All glory to God, who is able to keep you from falling away and will bring you with great joy into his glorious presence without a single fault. —JUDE 1:24, NLT
I don't know if I can go on.	Take My yoke upon you and learn from Me, for I am gentle and humble in heart, and YOU WILL FIND REST FOR YOUR SOULS. For My yoke is easy and My burden is light. —MATTHEW 11:29–30

THE ENEMY'S LIE	GOD'S TRUTH— OUR DEFENSE
I think God is punishing me.	God has not destined us for wrath, but for obtaining salvation through our Lord Jesus Christ, who died for us, so that whether we are awake or asleep, we will live together with Him. —1 THESSALONIANS 5:9–10
God couldn't possibly forgive *what I have done.*	If we confess our sins, He is faithful and righteous to forgive us our sins and to cleanse us from all unrighteousness. —1 JOHN 1:9
God couldn't possibly forget *what I have done.*	As far as the east is from the west, so far has He removed our transgressions from us. —PSALM 103:12

THE ENEMY'S LIE	GOD'S TRUTH— OUR DEFENSE
God couldn't possibly love me after what I have done.	God demonstrates His own love toward us, in that while we were yet sinners, Christ died for us. —ROMANS 5:8

Father, how grateful I am that You free me from false guilt and love me unconditionally. What a wonderful, comforting assurance that because of the substitutionary death of Christ on the cross, I can never lose my relationship with You—You will always love me. Thank You for being faithful to forgive my sins and cleanse me from unrighteousness as I confess my transgressions to You.

Father, when I feel false guilt, please help me to understand the cause of it so I can root it out. When I stray from Your will, help me to know immediately so I may repent—turning back to Your path for me. Lord, I choose to believe in Your full forgiveness, despite what I may feel. Help me to accept any consequences of my rebellion against You with grace and understanding.

Father, I know You can work all things together for good

for those who love You and are called according to Your purpose. Therefore, Lord, please help me learn from my mistakes and work through me to warn others of the dangers of sin. Lord God, make me an instrument of Your peace so that others will be drawn to Jesus as their Savior.

In Jesus' name I pray. Amen.

QUESTIONS FOR
PERSONAL REFLECTION AND GROUP STUDY

1. What can you do when you begin feeling unnecessary guilt over things you have no control of?

2. Can you think of a recent situation that paralyzed you with feelings of self-blame? Have you been able to overcome that guilt? What finally broke through your distorted thought patterns?

3. Have you ever felt the Holy Spirit prompting you to return to the center of God's will? How was His conviction of guilt different from your self-imposed feelings of condemnation?

4. Do you ever experience feelings of blame without a specific reason for them? What do you think could be causing this false guilt? What messages are connected with those feelings?

5. Is there anything stopping you from allowing Christ

to set you free from vicious strongholds that keep you in bondage? If so, what is it? Why is it important to you?

6. Do you identify with any of the examples from this chapter? Which one? What principles can you draw from that example to help renew your thinking?

7. Is there an area of your life in which you repeatedly feel shame and condemnation? What have you learned about allowing God to release you from it?

9

DESPAIR

Finding the Light of Hope in the Darkest Hour

ON A RECENT INTERNATIONAL TRIP, I had a layover in a city that turned out to be extremely cold and humid. Already wearied and weakened from extensive traveling, I developed a case of bronchitis that I just couldn't seem to shake, no matter how much rest I got or how many antibiotics I took. Within no time, that persistent respiratory infection turned into a dangerous case of pneumonia, and I found myself flat on my back in a hospital. I felt very weak and somewhat helpless. When the physician came in to tell me that it would be a while before I'd be released from the hospital, I was absolutely disheartened.

That was not where I wanted to be, of course. More than ever I longed to preach the gospel and teach people how to know Christ as their Savior. I was turning eighty and celebrating fifty-five years in the ministry—milestones I had anticipated with great joy and expectancy. Likewise, at In Touch Ministries, we were commemorating our thirty-fifth anniversary of broadcasting the Good News of salvation and were in absolute awe of all the astounding doors of opportunity our awesome God was opening for us to reach even more lost souls. I had plans to make; speaking engagements to attend; my photo book, *I Love to Tell the Story,* to finish editing; sermons to preach; and new places to see. I could not be sick. There was too much to accomplish. There was too much I knew the Father still wanted me to do to help others know Him. But I couldn't do any of it because I had no energy.

Impatiently, I waited to get better, but it seemed like my condition only deteriorated. Some of the medication actually worsened my ailment, rather than improve it. And from lying on my back with the pneumonia, I began to develop two agonizing pinched nerves in my back, which persisted for months. Eventually, the wear and tear on my body, inability to improve, and pain took its toll. I became downright despondent—dejected to a point of almost sheer despair.

You see, it occurred to me that I might miss out on everything. I thought about disappointing loved ones, friends, and partners in ministry and failing to take hold of important opportunities that we would never be able to regain. Even worse, I considered the devastating possibility that I would no longer be able to carry out my calling. I couldn't help it, of course, but I felt like I was letting everyone down—especially God. So much joy, effective service, and fruitfulness was within my reach, but I just could not grasp it. I had absolutely no control over my situation.

When you are flat on your back in pain and disheartenment, up is the only way you can look.

I had never experienced those feelings to the profound degree I had them those few days. I understand what it feels like to be so low that you can barely look up. Still, when you are flat on your back in pain and disheartenment, up is the only way you can look.

I frankly didn't have much energy or desire to pray, but I made myself focus on God, knowing He was my only hope and comfort. I cried out to Him to heal me and free me from the darkness of the emotions I was feeling. And He did. What the Father eventually showed me through that difficult experience was this: *Despair is a spiritual battle that you and I must choose to fight.*

> *Despair is a spiritual battle that you and I must choose to fight.*

I often say, "Disappointments are inevitable, but discouragement is a choice." And it is true. But you and I both know that there are devastating times in our lives that stretch everything we know and believe. We are in pain—at times physically, at other times emotionally, and sometimes both. Some of these seasons last much longer than a few days, and the physical strain can take a terrible toll on our emotions. Conversely—when we are continuously despondent and disheartened, our bodies can suffer as well. Frustrations and setbacks bombard us at an alarming rate, undermining our every confidence. Just when we think we will get better, more bad news hits us.

We wonder why God would allow all the agony we are experiencing. We ask, "Why me, Lord? Why now?" At the same time, the enemy is doing his best to make us question whether the Father really loves us—bringing up old sins, faults, and mistakes that have already been forgiven, and insinuating they disqualify us from the Lord's blessings. What makes it even worse is that joy is just outside our reach—and we have no hope of taking hold of it. The sense of loss, helplessness, futility, and dissatisfaction with ourselves can be absolutely overwhelming.

THE FREQUENT COMPANION OF OTHER DAMAGED EMOTIONS

Have you ever experienced this? Have you faced the dark depths of despair—wondering if you'll ever climb out? Perhaps you feel this way now as you fight to overcome other damaged emotions.

I address this with you at this point in the book because as you struggle to overcome fear, rejection, bitterness, and guilt, you may be in awe at how your difficulties have *increased*—hitting you right where you hurt. Your emotions may seem like a raw, open wound, and you may feel profoundly discouraged that you do not yet have victory over your damaging emotions.

Most of all, you may be wondering, *Why isn't the Father helping me? I am trying to serve Him. Why has this situation only gotten worse instead of better? Why doesn't He heal me?* You cry out to Him and He comforts you, but the trial does not end and you cannot understand what He is doing. So you question, *Has the Lord failed? Am I so far gone and so intensely damaged that He cannot help me?*

No, my friend, the Father has not failed you. And the fact that He is still working on you is evidence that not only does He see your great potential, but He also desires to touch the world through you in an astounding way (Heb. 12:4–11).

Believe it or not, what you are experiencing is absolutely normal—and a necessary part of liberating you of the pain you feel. You see, adversity is not only a bridge to a deeper relationship with God; it is also the path to freedom and healing. Like a surgeon who expertly cuts out cancer, He must pierce you right where the concentration of pain is—right where the decay lies within you. So He uses trials as His precise scalpel—making meticulous and skillful incisions into your life

> *Adversity is not only a bridge to a deeper relationship with God; it is also the path to freedom and healing.*

that are agonizing, to be sure, but also absolutely necessary in order for you to be fully free of what is destroying you (Jer. 18:3–4).

Paul expressed this truth in 2 Corinthians 1:8–9 when he wrote, "We do not want you to be unaware, brethren, of our affliction which came to us in Asia, that we were burdened excessively, beyond our strength, so that we despaired even of life; indeed, we had the sentence of death within ourselves so that we would not trust in ourselves, but in God who raises the dead." Even the great apostle Paul faced terrible trials that were beyond his power to endure. Yet he saw the value in the trial—"so that we would not trust in ourselves, but in God who raises the dead" (v. 9).

Is there no easier way? You may wonder, *He is God; why does He allow it to be so painful?* The simple truth is that we learn more in the difficulties of life than in the blessings. Through our hardships, He removes the thought patterns, habits, attitudes, behaviors, and even the relationships that allow us to depend on anything other than Him. Trials drive us to our knees in prayer, stop us from relying on ourselves, and teach us His all-sufficiency. As I said, when you are flat on your back with no other options, your only choice is to look up.

Yet it is in looking to Him that we ultimately have the greatest hope, joy, peace, and freedom. The prophet Isaiah testifies, "Although the Lord has given you bread of privation and water of oppression, He, your Teacher will no longer hide Himself, but your eyes will behold your Teacher. Your ears will hear a word behind you, 'This is the way, walk in it,' whenever you turn to the right or to the left" (Isa. 30:20–21). When you are able to rely on Him fully, you recognize that regardless of what circumstances you face, your Teacher—your omnipotent, omniscient, omnipresent, and unconditionally loving God—is there to guide you, protect you, and provide for you perfectly.

> *It is in looking to Him that we ultimately have the greatest hope, joy, peace, and freedom.*

THE CHALLENGE OF CHOICE

The challenge, of course, is that you must make the choice to trust Him. You must look beyond the painful circumstances—all the evidence you can see, feel, smell, hear, and touch—and realize there is a greater unseen reality, which is the presence of the

Living God (2 Cor. 4:16–18). This is not easy, but takes a constant refocus and realignment of your thinking. Everything in your spirit may fight against it, and with good reason. How can you trust one whom you cannot experience with your five senses? Yet to do otherwise is no option at all—the consequences of discouragement are just too great.

1. A Negative Inward Focus

First, despair generally causes a person to turn inward and dwell on whatever is disheartening him—perhaps a failure, loss, or frustration that undermines all his hopes and dreams. Now the individual may not be expressing this outright, but he knows something is off in his heart. He senses his troubled mood and thinks, *God, what is the matter with me? Why do I feel so sad and overwhelmed?* This silent prayer is repeated frequently until the message takes hold in his inner being—something is wrong; he is both desolate and defeated.

The mind, of course, looks for reasons for his pain and finds them in the individual's faults, limitations, and sins. It grabs hold of everything negative that touches his life, searching for meaning. Whether he struggles with fear, rejection, bitterness, or guilt, he begins reciting the negative messages to himself, which then exacerbates the underlying emotions and deepens his discouragement. He loses all perspective on his situation or how it really compares with the suffering of others.

2. A Poor Testimony

Second, remaining in a constant state of despair can undermine your witness. The enemy knows he can do nothing to harm your soul. Jesus promised in John 10:27–29, "My sheep hear My voice, and I know them, and they follow Me; and I give eternal life to them, and they will never perish; and *no one will snatch them out of My hand.* My Father, who has given them to Me, *is greater than all; and no one is able to snatch them out of the Father's hand"* (emphasis added). Once you accept Jesus as your Savior, the evil one has absolutely no way to alter your eternal destiny.

However, the enemy *can* damage your testimony and squelch your effectiveness for the kingdom of God—and so he makes this his goal. After all, "We are His workmanship, created in Christ Jesus for good works, which God prepared beforehand so that we would walk in them" (Eph. 2:10). The devil realizes if he can prevent you from embracing what the Father fashioned you to be, he can then stop you from discovering what would give your life true significance and meaning.

How does he do so? As we have seen, he may use fear or turn you against yourself with feelings of guilt. He may tempt you to turn away from God through unbelief. He may even entice you to dull your sorrows with illicit substances, sexual exploits, or other destructive behaviors.

Now, the inherent message of Christianity is "Believe in the Lord Jesus, and you will be saved" (Acts 16:31). But if a person is continuously plagued with negative thoughts, guilt, and despondency, then the lost and dying world will not see the liberty that comes from having your sins forgiven, the comfort and hope that result from being reconciled to the Lord, and the joy of an eternal home in heaven with Him. There will be nothing to recommend Jesus to the unbeliever.

3. Self-Destructive Actions

Third, you may seek to alleviate your soul in ways that will actually increase your bondage and deepen your desolation. In fact, when you are profoundly discouraged, you may pursue activities to ease your woundedness that do not make sense, even to yourself.

Like those plagued with guilt, you may try to take control of the situation by punishing yourself.

Perhaps you push away your loved ones—and especially God—in order to avoid more rejection or condemnation. It is possible that you could endeavor to establish stability and order in your life through obsessive attention to what you eat, cleaning, or exercise. You may be tempted to seek refuge in earthly comforts such as attaining wealth or engaging in sinful behaviors. You may even throw yourself more deeply into ministry, work, or a hobby in order to hide your hurt, only to become more wounded when they do not lessen your grief and the trials of life disillusion you further.

Friend, many things will promise relief for your hurting soul, but do not be fooled—they will not satisfy the deep longing within you. Only God can heal your suffering. All other pursuits will only result in even more pain, because they will continue to reinforce the false messages you believe about yourself.

Now, before we move forward, I would like to make an important distinction. What we have been discussing is the discouragement and despair that all of us face at one point or another. In fact, because of circumstances beyond their control—such as an abusive relationship, ongoing physical pain, residing in a nation embroiled in war, or what have you—some people may face devastating disheartenment quite often.

However, there comes a point when a person moves beyond a despondent mood to what is known to professional psychologists as *clinical depression*—which may result from a long-term biological condition that is not necessarily related to what is happening in the person's life or the choices he or she makes. At times, such a condition is accompanied by symptoms such as substantial weight gain or loss, insomnia or hypersomnia, cognitive problems, and even hallucinations.

As I indicated in the second chapter, the precious souls who suffer from true chemical imbalances should seek professional help and may sometimes even require medication to help correct what is occurring in them biologically. If this is you, I want you to know the Father loves you and there is hope for you. I strongly encourage you to seek support and find a godly, Christian counselor who can offer the help you need. But in addition to professional assistance, make every effort to employ the principles outlined in this chapter. God is your ultimate source of help and healing, and trusting Him is vital to your recovery.

4. A Desire to Quit—Permanently

I say all of this in lieu of the fourth consequence of despair, which is that the person may feel as if there is no use continuing with the burdens he bears, so he walks away from his calling, goals, vocation, and/or even his family. Regardless of the reality of his situation, the only thing he can focus on is the abiding sense that no one cares about him; there is none who appreciate or help him; and he has no reason to fight anymore. He has lost his motivation, his will, and his purpose. Ultimately, a severely dejected person may even come to the conclusion that his only option is suicide.

Sadly, this happens a great deal more often than we may believe. In fact, the Centers for Disease Control and Prevention reports that more people in the United States die from taking their own lives than from automobile accidents.[1]

Of course, the reasons are as numerous as the people who attempt it.

- As we saw with the Japanese kamikaze pilots of World War II and the terrorists on September 11, 2001, sometimes people take their own lives because of a cause they believe in. Perhaps they are promised rewards or some type of recognition in exchange for their lives.

---

[1] Centers for Disease Control and Prevention, *Morbidity and Mortality Weekly Report*, vol. 62, no. 17, May 3, 2013, http://www.cdc.gov/mmwr/pdf/wk/mm6217.pdf.

- Sometimes people feel as though they are simply going through the motions in their lives—they cannot find meaning or purpose to sustain them, and therefore believe they have no valid reason to continue on.

- As we just discussed, some people suffer from long-term despondency and biochemical imbalances that drive them to feel as if they have no choices. A future trapped in such despondency can seem so bleak that they long for a way of escape.

- People can also face circumstances that seem hopeless—especially if they feel continuous and unbearable pain, experience a terrible financial reversal, or lose loved ones. With no relief from their burdens in view, they believe suicide is their only way out.

- At times, an elderly couple that has been together a long time will have a love pact—they decide that after thirty, forty, or fifty years of marriage, for example, they do not wish to live without the other. So when one of the spouses becomes ill or debilitated, they take their lives together.

- And then there are those who commit suicide out of retaliation or vengeance toward another person who has harmed or betrayed them.

People have many reasons, but is suicide ever a course of action God approves of? No, it is not. We can look back at the Sixth Commandment in Exodus 20:13 and see that God's Word is clear:

"You shall not murder." The word used in the Hebrew is *râtsach* and it can apply to killing oneself.

In fact, nowhere does the Bible condone suicide. Why? Because it is a form of escape, an expression of unbelief, an act of utter self-hatred. In essence, the person who takes his or her life is saying, "I don't believe the Lord can help me with this terrible problem. I don't think He will answer my prayers or that He even loves me. I doubt all of it—so I will take my life into my own hands." In doing so, they usurp His authority and become god in His place, feigning to hold the keys of life and death (Rev. 1:18).

Is this ever an attitude that honors the Father? Absolutely not. Friend, there is *always* hope in God, regardless of how difficult and unbearable your circumstances may seem (Lam. 3:19–25). You cannot name one trial that is greater than His power to overcome it. He can lead you to victory no matter what you face.

> *Friend, there is always hope in God, no matter how difficult and unbearable your circumstances may seem.*

Therefore, if you ever get to the point where you wonder if life is worth living, please seek help. Your life is important—you are worthwhile. Explain what you are feeling to a trusted pastor, godly counselor, family member, or friend who can support you and walk with you through the dark times you face. If you don't know whom to turn to, go to a local Bible-believing church, call a Christian Counseling Center, or seek out a Christ-centered ministry. Do not remain silent about your pain. You do not have to—and should not—fight this battle alone.

Now, before we move on, let me clear up a misconception I frequently hear repeated.

If you or someone you love has attempted suicide, please be assured that it is not the unpardonable sin. Some believe it is because the person does not have the opportunity to repent, but nothing in God's Word suggests suicide will not be forgiven.

As we discussed in Chapter 5, the only unpardonable sin is "blasphemy against the Spirit" (Matt. 12:31), which is the outright rejection of Christ as Savior through continued unbelief. Although the Holy Spirit convicts you of your need for salvation, you refuse His promptings and decline Jesus' perfect provision at the cross and through His resurrection. But the person who dies "in Christ" (Rom. 3:24), who is "sealed in Him with the Holy Spirit of promise" (Eph. 1:13), will be saved, even if he has no opportunity to confess before he dies.

> *Even though suicide is not the unpardonable sin, its consequences are still absolutely devastating.*

Of course, it is also important for us to understand that even though suicide is not the unpardonable sin, its consequences are still absolutely devastating.

Not only does suicide bring excruciating and long-term pain to the individual's loved ones; but it also plagues them with questions that can never be answered. I've spoken to many family members who just cannot understand what happened. Often, they are tortured with thoughts such as, *How did I miss the fact she was hurting so much? Did I say or do something that wounded her? Didn't she realize how*

*much we love her? Why didn't she say anything about how she was feel-
ing? If she had just told me, I would have helped in some way—in any
way within my power—to get her through her pain. I just wish there
was something I could have done to stop her from destroying herself.*

The agony they endure does not go away because they are always left wondering, *Why?* And, *Was there anything I could have
done differently?*

*Suicide also means that the person forfeits God's plans for their
lives.* The Lord may have some very important things for that person to accomplish and may be teaching profound lessons through
his adversity.

For example, one of England's great seventeenth-century
authors, John Donne, struggled with terrible physical ailments,
poverty, and depression. In fact, five of his twelve children died
young—two were stillborn and the others perished early in their
youth. He experienced losses few people could bear.

However, Donne did not turn his back on God or take his life;
rather, he chose to cling to the Lord. In fact, as he struggled with
a terrible illness, he wrote Meditation XVII of his *Devotions upon
Emergent Occasions,* and affirmed: "Affliction is a treasure, and
scarce any man hath enough of it. No man hath affliction enough
that is not matured and ripened by and made fit for God by that
affliction. . . . Tribulation is treasure . . . we get nearer and nearer
our home, heaven, by it."

Donne understood that his adversity was a bridge to a deeper
relationship with the Father. Therefore, he did not give up when

tempted to despair. Rather, he embraced the difficulties for the good they could bring him. And because of his faith, the Church of England still celebrates his life four hundred years later, on March 31 of every year.

> *He embraced the difficulties for the good they could bring him.*

Think of all a person could miss if he decides to take his life. If Joseph had given up at his lowest point, he would not have enjoyed the honor of being Pharaoh's second in command. If Moses had yielded to his despondency, he wouldn't have led the people of Israel out of Egyptian bondage and to the Promised Land. And if David had committed suicide during those terrible moments when he knew Saul was pursuing him, he had no one to count on, and everything seemed utterly against him, he would never have become the great king of Israel and an ancestor to the Messiah, our Lord Jesus.

Likewise, the person who even considers suicide as an option must realize that God's deliverance may be just around the corner and that all his hopes may soon be fulfilled. But if he gives up and yields to the despair, then he will never discover what would have been possible with the Father's help.

So if the suffering soul would just hold on—express his faith and cling to almighty God, certainly his hope will be renewed and rewarded—just as it was for David, Moses, and Joseph.

This is why David testified, "I would have despaired unless I had believed that I would see the goodness of the LORD in the land of the living. Wait for the LORD; be strong and let your heart take courage; yes, wait for the LORD" (Ps. 27:13–14). He understood that when God is with you, there is no such thing as a truly hopeless situation. The best thing to do is wait to see what He will do, trusting that He will help you.

When God is with you, there is no such thing as a truly hopeless situation.

So let me ask you: Have you ever considered doing harm to yourself? Have you ever lamented, *Life is not worth living. I just want to die.* Whether or not you seriously contemplate taking your life, I would ask that whenever your thoughts turn dark and dangerous, that you would remember that the Father knows all about your situation and He's committed to helping you overcome it. He loves you just as you are, and He is willing to walk with you step by step through whatever suffering and sorrow you face.

Therefore, take heart—you have almighty God on your side. Invite Him into your life as your Redeemer, Deliverer, Protector, Provider, and Friend. Think about the astounding privilege it is that you can count on Him, and allow it to comfort your aching soul. You can let go of your despair and look forward to the future. You will most likely be absolutely astounded at the plans your heavenly Father has for you.

THE DECISION TO TRUST

Of course, you may be tempted to beat yourself up and question if you really know the Lord at all. The enemy's messages play in your mind, *Christians shouldn't have such dark and discouraged thoughts. What is wrong with me? I must not really have a relationship with God if I am so depressed. All of God's promises are for other people—not for me.*

If at any point those thoughts enter your mind, rebuke the enemy immediately and turn to Scripture. There are few saints in God's Word who did not face some form of despair. Their victory wasn't that they were always cheerful. Rather, they triumphed because they knew Who to turn to whenever discouragement assailed their souls.

- For example, David declared, "Why are you in despair, O my soul? And why are you disturbed within me? Hope in God, for I shall again praise Him, the help of my countenance and my God" (Ps. 43:5).
- Likewise, the prophet Habakkuk testified, "Though the fig tree should not blossom and there be no fruit on the vines, though the yield of the olive should fail and the fields produce no food, though the flock should be cut off from the fold and there be no cattle in the stalls, yet I will exult in the LORD, I will rejoice in the God of my salvation. The Lord GOD is my strength" (Hab. 3:17–19).
- When faced with the onslaught of three overwhelmingly powerful armies, King Jehoshaphat affirmed, "We are powerless before this great multitude who are coming against us; nor do we know what to do, but our eyes are on You" (2 Chron. 20:12).

- Even the Lord Jesus faced a time of terrible desperation at Gethsemane and said, "My soul is deeply grieved, to the point of death" (Matt. 26:38). Scripture tells us that He prayed not once, nor twice—but He sought the Father *three times* during that terrible hour. If the perfect, sinless Son of the Living God— God Himself—went repeatedly to the throne of grace for comfort as He faced such devastating emotions, what does that say to us? Not only are those feelings a reality to all of us, but we can and should go often to the Father's arms for compassion, mercy, and consolation.

Another prime example of this is the great prophet Elijah, who defied and defeated wicked King Ahab and 850 prophets of the false deities Baal and Asherah on Mount Carmel (1 Kings 18:16– 40). We know Elijah was a man of extraordinary faith because Scripture recounts how he bravely challenged the 450 prophets of Baal, saying:

"How long will you hesitate between two opinions? If the LORD is God, follow Him; but if Baal, follow him . . . I alone am left a prophet of the LORD, but Baal's prophets are 450 men. Now let them give us two oxen; and let them choose one ox for themselves and cut it up, and place it on the wood, but put no fire under it; and I will prepare the other ox and lay it on the wood, and I will not put a fire under it. Then you call on the name of your god, and I will call on the name of the LORD, and the God who answers by fire, He is God" (vv. 21–24).

The false prophets prayed loudly for hours, cutting themselves with swords and spears so their blood would attract Baal's notice. But 1 Kings 18:26 confirms, "There was no voice and no one answered." Impotent and useless, Baal sent no fire.

Elijah was unafraid. He increased the difficulty of the task by soaking the offering with so much water that it filled a large trench. Then he called out to the Great I AM—*Yahweh*, the God of Israel. Again, Scripture tells us, "Then the fire of the LORD fell and consumed the burnt offering and the wood and the stones and the dust, and licked up the water that was in the trench. When all the people saw it, they fell on their faces; and they said, 'The LORD, He is God; the LORD, He is God'" (1 Kings 18:38–39). It was a tremendous display of the Father's power and an astounding spiritual victory for Elijah.

One would think a man of God with so much faith and who had experienced such an overwhelming triumph over his enemies would never reach the point of hopeless despondency or fear defeat. Yet that is exactly what happened. And it wasn't a terrifying army, powerful rulers, natural disasters, or extraordinary losses that caused him to feel utterly hopeless and helpless. It was a threat by a woman, Jezebel, the wife of King Ahab.

She sent a message to him saying, "May the gods strike me and even kill me if by this time tomorrow I have not killed you just as you killed them" (1 Kings 19:2, NLT).

First Kings 19:3–4 (NLT) reports, "Elijah was afraid and fled for his life . . . He went on alone into the wilderness, traveling all day. He sat down under a solitary broom tree and prayed that he might die. 'I have had enough, LORD,' he said. 'Take my life, for I am no better than my ancestors who have already died.'"

Elijah—one of the greatest, most courageous and influential prophets Israel had ever known—was absolutely terrified and utterly depressed. Exhausted and overwhelmed by uncertainty, he asked God to kill him. He simply did not want to live anymore.

Yet, God was gracious and tender with the weary prophet, just as He is with you. He understood Elijah's discouragement and ministered to him in a wonderful way.

1. The Father Cared for Elijah's Physical Needs

It is amazing how being rundown from hunger, weariness, loneliness, and frustration can affect the emotions. Likewise, there may be other bodily factors that influence how we feel—such as how the pneumonia and pinched nerves I experienced disheartened me. Elijah was probably so exhausted, famished, and isolated that he lost heart and gave in to fear. Yet the Lord sent him help. We're told, "There was an angel touching him, and he said to him, 'Arise, eat'" (1 Kings 19:5).

2. God Brought Elijah to Safety

First Kings 19:8 reports, "He arose and ate and drank, and went in the strength of that food forty days and forty nights to Horeb, the mountain of God." Horeb—also known as Mount Sinai—was more than two hundred miles from the evil queen's grasp, which must have given Elijah some comfort. But it was also where the Lord had established His covenant with Israel and had given the Ten Commandments to His servant Moses (Ex. 19:16—20:18).

In other words, this was not only a place of physical security for the prophet; it was also a landmark of spiritual significance. Just as the Father had successfully defeated the Egyptians and brought His people faithfully to this mountain, so He could protect Elijah and vanquish Queen Jezebel. Likewise, whenever we are discouraged, it is important to seek out a place of safety, take refuge in the Lord, and remember all the ways He has been faithful in the past.

3. God Changed Elijah's Focus

When Elijah arrived at Horeb, the Father commanded the prophet to stand before Him. First Kings 19:11–13 reports,

> Behold, the LORD was passing by! And a great and strong wind was rending the mountains and breaking in pieces the rocks before the LORD; but the LORD was not in the wind. And after the wind an earthquake, but the LORD was not in the earthquake. After the earthquake a fire, but the LORD was not in the fire; and after the fire a sound of a gentle blowing. When Elijah heard it, he wrapped his face in his mantle and went out and stood in the entrance of the cave.

Elijah was so intently centered on his problems with Jezebel that he was missing the obvious: as a servant of the living God, he had absolutely nothing to fear. The sovereign King of creation—who could command the winds, cause the earth to tremble, and send fire—was the One who would always faithfully help him (Ps. 103:17–19).

So the Lord reminded Elijah of one of the most important principles any of us will ever learn: *Whenever problems arise, get alone and listen quietly for God.* Take time to intentionally kneel in silence before His holy presence. He will speak to you. Dwelling on your problem will never make it go away, but focusing on the Father is always the pathway to success.

4. God Commissioned Elijah

The Lord told Elijah, "Go, return on your way to the wilderness of Damascus, and when you have arrived, you shall anoint Hazael king over Aram; and Jehu the son of Nimshi you shall anoint king over Israel; and Elisha the son of Shaphat of Abel-meholah you shall anoint as prophet in your place" (1 Kings 19:15–16). The Lord knew that what the prophet needed was a new sense of purpose.

Though Elijah had experienced glorious victory on Mount Carmel, it must have been both frustrating and disappointing that Ahab and Jezebel were still ruling Israel and refusing to repent. What was the use of doing such mighty things for God if nothing really changed?

Yet by giving the prophet this commission, the Father was telling him that hope was not gone, but that a new stage of His perfect plan was about to commence. Through Hazael, Jehu, and Elisha, the Lord would ensure that justice was done and that Ahab and Jezebel would be held accountable. And sure enough, all that the Lord promised came to pass (1 Kings 22:34–39; 2 Kings 9:30–37).

5. God Gave Elijah a Support System

Twice in this encounter, Elijah lamented, "I alone am left" (1 Kings 19:10, 14), betraying his feelings of isolation, fear, and loneliness. So the Lord's final point was to assure the prophet that he would not be alone. "I will leave 7,000 in Israel, all the knees that have not bowed to Baal" (1 Kings 19:18). No doubt, in our struggles we often feel the same way. Yet the Father assures us that we have not been abandoned on this journey and He will never call us to go it alone.

Elijah was able to make the choice to fight despair by trusting God. Though trials would continue to arise in this tumultuous period of Israel's history, the prophet had steadfast faith in the Lord's faithful provision. You can, too. Like Elijah, you can hold on to God no matter what happens or how discouraging your situation may become—knowing that your greatest moments of victory are often preceded by moments of seemingly insurmountable defeat.

HOPE FOR YOU

As I said in the beginning of this chapter, adversity is the Lord's best tool for delivering you from the bondage of damaged emotions. Through our troubles He can replace our faulty thought patterns with His own; purge us of ungodly habits, attitudes, and behaviors; and teach us to rely on His perfect strength, wisdom, and love. However, you have an important choice in this—you must decide whether you will allow hope to rule your life or continue to allow despair to dominate you.

If you permit negativity and despondency to characterize your life, then every time there is a new problem or obstacle, it will deepen your dejection and cause you further pain.

But if you will view each difficulty and challenge that comes to you as an opportunity to learn more about your heavenly Father, draw closer to Him in loving fellowship, and be cleansed from your bondage to sin, I guarantee your life will be absolutely transformed (1 Pet. 1:6–7).

View each difficulty and challenge that comes to you as an opportunity to draw closer to your heavenly Father.

This was certainly true for Charles Haddon Spurgeon, the great nineteenth-century Baptist preacher from England. Spurgeon was a man who knew deep agony and despair. Plagued by rheumatic gout and kidney disease, he often experienced so much pain that he could not leave his house. Because of these infirmities, the disability of his beloved wife, Susannah, extreme poverty, unyielding criticism, and other debilitating trials, Spurgeon frequently dealt with terrible bouts of depression—with good reason. Yet Spurgeon never allowed the feelings of despair to stop him from preaching. In fact, he was able to see the immensely positive value of struggling with such profound feelings and entrusting them to the Father. He wrote,

> This depression comes over me whenever the Lord is preparing a larger blessing for my ministry; the cloud is black before it breaks, and overshadows before it yields its deluge of mercy. Depression has now become to me as a prophet in rough clothing, a John the Baptist, heralding the nearer coming of my Lord's richer benison. So have far better men found it. The scouring of the vessel has fitted it for the Master's use. Immersion in suffering has preceded the baptism of the Holy Ghost. Fasting gives an appetite for the banquet. The Lord is revealed in the backside of the desert, while his servant keepeth the sheep and waits in solitary awe. The wilderness is the way to Canaan. The low valley leads to the towering mountain. Defeat prepares for victory.[2]

Because Spurgeon was willing to allow adversity to be God's tool of refinement in his life, the Lord made him extremely fruitful. It is estimated that he preached more than 3,500 sermons and was able to teach close to 10 million people—an astounding accomplishment considering he did not have the modern-day con-

---

[2] Charles Haddon Spurgeon, "The Minister's Fainting Fits, Lectures to My Students, Lecture XI," 1856.

veniences of radio and television to help spread the message and that he died at the young age of fifty-seven.

Like Spurgeon, perhaps you have devastating difficulties that seem to hold you captive. If so, then at this point I ask you to make a conscious choice to trust the Lord your God to transform your circumstances. Allow Him to change the way you think so you can break free from your discouragement and use your adversity as a conduit for knowing Him better. No doubt the most significant seasons of spiritual growth will correspond with the hardest challenges you experience.

But how do you do so? How do you maintain your trust in God when you face difficulties and distresses?

1. *Allow Signs of Despair to Lead You to Prayer*

The emotions you're experiencing are a warning sign to your spirit revealing that you need to turn to God. He is calling you—drawing you into a relationship with Him. Go to Him with an open heart and invite Him to teach you. Ask the Father, "What is it You desire to accomplish in and through me?" Then open your Bible before Him and allow Him to guide you to the truth He desires to teach you.

2. *Take Stock of Your Life*

Are you struggling with weariness, frustration, isolation, or are you eating an unhealthy diet? This may be adding to your despair. Don't allow the enemy to get a foothold. Rather, remember the acrostic HALT—whenever you're Hungry, Angry, Lonely, or Tired, remember to stop, refuel, and seek the Lord's guidance. God will encourage your heart and give you the ability to endure whatever trouble you may face. And if you face trials, difficulties, or emotions that are too overwhelming to handle on your own, seek godly believers who will support and help you.

3. Commit Yourself to Your Father's Plans

Did you know that one of the biggest gold deposits that was ever excavated in the United States was discovered two inches beneath where a previous miner had given up? We make a terrible mistake when we decide to quit because we fear our circumstances will never change. But friend, God has wonderful plans for your future!

> *Cling to the Lord with all your heart, mind, soul, and strength regardless of what happens, with the knowledge that He ultimately provides what is absolutely best for you.*

I cannot stress enough how important it is to cling to the Lord with all your heart, mind, soul, and strength regardless of what happens, with the knowledge that He ultimately provides what is absolutely best for you. The truth of the matter is, sometimes you will not understand why the Father allows certain challenges to touch your life, but with God there is always hope. And there are abundant blessings that you will forfeit if you give in to your discouragement.

Don't miss out on the good things the Father has for you by submitting to despair. Rather, claim Psalm 30:5, "Weeping may last for the night, but a shout of joy comes in the morning." Devote yourself to the Lord. Keep focused on staying in the center of His will and fulfilling His plans for your life, because He will certainly strengthen you to go on.

4. Embrace Who God Says You Are

Often, when we struggle with despair, experience loss, or fail at something important, we attribute our painful feelings to our own sense of worth. We believe that we don't deserve acceptance or anything good, and it is very difficult to break out of those beliefs because they are so intrinsic to our identity.

However, you must accept the reality that how you view yourself is not who you really are. Your perception is incorrect. Rather, the only One who truly understands your potential and worth is the Father, who accepts you, promises to love you unconditionally, and enables you to do all He calls you to do.

Your job is not to defend your limitations or make excuses for your faults. Rather, your responsibility is to take your eyes completely off of what you can accomplish and focus your full attention on Him (2 Cor. 12:7–10).

Zephaniah 3:17 affirms, "The LORD your God is in your midst, a victorious warrior. He will exult over you with joy, He will be quiet in His love, He will rejoice over you with shouts of joy." Your heavenly Father is committed to winning the battles for you (Ex. 14:14). Therefore, train your eyes on Him, obey His commands, and accept who He created you to be—a vessel who shines with His glory.

5. *Praise the Lord*

As I indicated before, you have two choices when you face discouraging circumstances. You can focus on the problems, which will cause you greater despair. Or you can look to God and praise Him for what He is—your absolutely sure Foundation, Everlasting Hope, Mighty Warrior, Perfect Provider, Beloved Counselor, Sovereign King of kings, Incomparable Protector, Great Physician, and Unfailing Friend.

You see, dejection and praise cannot coexist in your heart for very long. Because when you gaze on the abundant goodness and mercy of the Father and you voice your sincere thankfulness and adoration to Him, there is no way to maintain a hopeless state. It is an absolute fact: praising God is a bulwark against despair.

6. *Do the Lord's Work*

We will cover this more in the final chapter, but it is important to understand that our suffering is never in vain. Adversity not only helps us to know God better but it also trains us for His service to others.

This is a principle we can find in 2 Corinthians 1:3–4, which proclaims, "Blessed be the God and Father of our Lord Jesus Christ, the Father of mercies and God of all comfort, who comforts us in all our affliction so that we will be able to comfort those who are in any affliction with the comfort with which we ourselves are comforted by God."

When you and I find victory over fear, rejection, bitterness, guilt and despair, we become ambassadors the Lord can work through to lead others to freedom. This is because we know how they feel, we can assure them they are not alone, and we will have compassion to walk with them as they pursue healing. An additional benefit of this, of course, is that while we are ministering to others, our focus is off our own troubles. Therefore, overcome your discouragement by offering yourself to God and allowing Him to do His awesome work through you.

> *When you and I find victory over fear, rejection, bitterness, guilt, and despair, we become ambassadors the Lord can work through to lead others to freedom.*

Friend, no matter what happens in your life, don't let go of the Savior. Despair doesn't have to keep you in its grip. You can defeat it by choosing to think about all the Father has given you and the great plans He has for your future.

So respond to your feelings of discouragement with prayer and your thoughts of defeat with truth from His Word. Commit yourself to trusting His plan regardless of the circumstances, claim His unfailing promises, cling to His loving presence, and lift your voice in praise to Him. Learn to see the adversity you face as a tool that the Lord is using to do something extraordinary in your life.

Then, even in the midst of disheartening challenges, you can be a victor who experiences His supernatural hope, strength, joy, and peace.

GOD'S TRUTH	OUR DEFENSE
For times when all outward evidence is against you.	Though the fig tree should not blossom and there be no fruit on the vines, though the yield of the olive should fail and the fields produce no food, though the flock should be cut off from the fold and there be no cattle in the stalls, yet I will exult in the LORD, I will rejoice in the God of my salvation. The Lord GOD is my strength. —HABAKKUK 3:17–19
For times when you wonder if any good comes from your suffering.	We know that God causes all things to work together for good to those who love God, to those who are called according to His purpose. —ROMANS 8:28

GOD'S TRUTH	OUR DEFENSE
For times of great pressure.	We are pressed on every side by troubles, but we are not crushed. We are perplexed, but not driven to despair. We are hunted down, but never abandoned by God. We get knocked down, but we are not destroyed. Through suffering, our bodies continue to share in the death of Jesus so that the life of Jesus may also be seen in our bodies. —2 CORINTHIANS 4:8–10, NLT

GOD'S TRUTH	OUR DEFENSE
For times when you need a reason to keep going.	We can rejoice, too, when we run into problems and trials, for we know that they help us develop endurance. And endurance develops strength of character, and character strengthens our confident hope of salvation. And this hope will not lead to disappointment. For we know how dearly God loves us, because he has given us the Holy Spirit to fill our hearts with his love. —ROMANS 5:3–5, NLT

GOD'S TRUTH	OUR DEFENSE
For times when others hurt you.	"Do not be afraid, for am I in God's place? As for you, you meant evil against me, but God meant it for good in order to bring about this present result, to preserve many people alive." —GENESIS 50:19–20
For times when you feel you have no one to come to your defense.	The Lord stood with me and strengthened me, so that through me the proclamation might be fully accomplished, and that all the Gentiles might hear; and I was rescued out of the lion's mouth. The Lord will rescue me from every evil deed, and will bring me safely to His heavenly kingdom; to Him be the glory forever and ever. Amen. —2 TIMOTHY 4:17–18

GOD'S TRUTH	OUR DEFENSE
For times when your enemies seem too numerous to handle.	When the enemy shall come in like a flood, the Spirit of the LORD shall lift up a standard against him. —ISAIAH 59:19, KJV
For times when you need wisdom.	If any of you lacks wisdom, let him ask of God, who gives to all generously and without reproach, and it will be given to him. —JAMES 1:5
For times when you fear you will not have enough.	He who did not spare His own Son, but delivered Him over for us all, how will He not also with Him freely give us all things? —ROMANS 8:32

GOD'S TRUTH	OUR DEFENSE
For times when you feel weak.	The Everlasting God, the LORD, the Creator of the ends of the earth does not become weary or tired. His understanding is inscrutable. He gives strength to the weary, and to him who lacks might He increases power. Though youths grow weary and tired, and vigorous young men stumble badly, yet those who wait for the LORD will gain new strength; they will mount up with wings like eagles, they will run and not get tired, they will walk and not become weary. —ISAIAH 40:28–31

GOD'S TRUTH	OUR DEFENSE
For when it seems like time is running out and there's no hope ahead.	For from days of old they have not heard or perceived by ear, nor has the eye seen a God besides You, who acts in behalf of the one who waits for Him. —ISAIAH 64:4
For times when you do not know what to pray.	The Spirit also helps our weakness; for we do not know how to pray as we should, but the Spirit Himself intercedes for us with groanings too deep for words; and He who searches the hearts knows what the mind of the Spirit is, because He intercedes for the saints according to the will of God. —ROMANS 8:26–27
For times when it seems like God will not keep His promises to you.	Not one word has failed of all His good promise. —1 KINGS 8:56

GOD'S TRUTH	OUR DEFENSE
For times when you fear you have no future.	"I know the plans that I have for you," declares the LORD, "plans for welfare and not for calamity to give you a future and a hope." —JEREMIAH 29:11

Father, how grateful I am that You understand when I feel disheartened and utterly hopeless. I give thanks for Your tenderness toward me and Your desire to heal my wounds. You know, Lord, how easy it is for me to become discouraged— even over the very trials You send to heal my damaged emotions. So Father, whenever I feel desolation rising up within me, help me to remember to kneel before You in prayer and seek Your loving face. Prompt me to renew my commitment to Your plans for my future and focus on Your matchless character. Help me to embrace who You've created me to be and may Your praises always be on my lips.

Lord, truly You are good—the holy, sovereign, and trustworthy God of all that exists. You are clothed with majesty and strength—Your wisdom none can fathom. Your unconditional love and astounding grace make my heart rejoice.

Thank You, Father, for giving me hope. Even when everything around me seems to be against me and there is no rescue in view, I know You are working on my behalf in the unseen. Truly, Your great and mighty plans are above and beyond all I could possibly ask or imagine. So help me be a vessel of Your glory—leading others to know You and helping them to find healing in Your unfailing presence.

Thank You, Father, for giving me the victory over despair and for making it the very classroom of learning where I can draw closer to You. In Jesus' wonderful name, I pray. Amen.

QUESTIONS FOR
PERSONAL REFLECTION AND GROUP STUDY

1. In what ways have you fought the debilitating emotion of despair?
2. How difficult is it to choose to trust God despite your circumstances? Why do you think it is so much easier to succumb to your natural feelings of defeat?
3. Have you ever felt as if your life were not worth living? What was the cause of your disheartenment?

4. What would you say to someone who feels that suicide is his only option?

5. Think of a recent time of adversity, what did you learn about the Lord through it? Did you see His activity in your life?

6. How have you seen adversity work as a bridge to a deeper relationship with God in your own life? Have you ever seen the Lord work through adversity to heal your emotions? Tell about your experience.

7. Have you experienced any great victories that were preceded by what seemed like overwhelming times of defeat?

8. Is there a situation you're dealing with today that feels absolutely overwhelming? What have you learned in this chapter about turning those crushing feelings of hopelessness over to the Lord?

Dear friend, if you, a group member, or someone you know voices feelings of ongoing despair or has considered committing suicide, please seek help. As I have said repeatedly in this chapter, God loves the hurting soul who needs His strength, comfort, and healing.

In fact, Psalm 34:18 tells us, "The LORD is near to the brokenhearted and saves those who are crushed in spirit." The Father has not and will not abandon people who are in deep pain. Rather, He is close to them—seeking them out and wanting to provide relief.

Therefore, please—if you, someone you know, or a member of your small group is suffering from depression or having suicidal thoughts, seek out a trusted counselor, pastor, family member, or godly friend for support. As I said before, do not remain silent when someone's life hangs in the balance. There is help and hope—so seek assistance as soon as possible.

10

ALL THE WAY TO VICTORY!

Looking Beyond Ourselves

THE FATHER HAS A PURPOSE for what you are experiencing. I can state that as a fact because it is a principle you can see throughout the pages of Scripture. The God who has numbered every hair on your head is intimately involved with the details of your life—even your emotions—and He cares for you deeply (Matt. 10:29–31). He understands the wounds you've sustained and how profoundly they have affected you. He knows the feelings you've struggled to overcome. And He also knows how to make all of it a beautiful testimony of His grace in your life (Isa. 61:3).

In fact, you are promised that not only can you triumph over the emotions you feel, He can make it an "overwhelming victory" for you (Rom. 8:37, TLB). Or as the King James Version says, you can be "more than [a] conqueror." In other words, the battle for control you've been fighting with your emotions has an even greater purpose if you are willing for Him to redeem it (Rom. 8:28).

I say this because throughout my own life I have seen that adversity can be God's greatest tool for our spiritual growth and continuing ministry to others. If we submit to Him in obedience and trust, He will renew our thoughts and place us firmly on His path for our lives—making us more fruitful than we perhaps thought possible.

Adversity can be God's greatest tool for our spiritual growth and continuing ministry to others.

I recall a particularly difficult season in my own life several years ago. It was a time similar to the one I told you about in Chapter 8, when I stretched myself too thin and tried to live up to untenable standards. During this particular period, I was preaching six times a week, taping two television programs, traveling across the nation, writing books, pastoring First Baptist Atlanta, and leading both the church staff and the employees at In Touch Ministries. It probably wouldn't surprise anyone that I was completely drained all of the time.

My exhaustion escalated and eventually I ended up in the hospital for a week—and completely out of circulation for three months. I felt as if I had been driving ninety miles an hour and had suddenly hit a brick wall. I could not preach, teach, go to meetings, make decisions, solve problems, or even visit with people. I couldn't do anything.

At first, I felt helpless and had to wrestle with my need to make sure everything was perfectly in order. But let me encourage you by saying that those three months ended up being extremely important to my relationship with the Father. He taught me that I was so occupied doing His work that I was actually missing His voice. I was not taking time to listen to Him. This lesson has made all the difference in my life and ministry. Likewise, your adversity can be a bridge to a deeper, more intimate relationship with God if you will pay attention to what He is teaching you.

A GOOD DECISION

In the previous chapter, I challenged you to make a choice: to look at the emotions you feel and the suffering you experience as an opportunity to embrace rather than as a cause for despondency. It would be helpful for you to know the wonderful fruit that comes from making such a decision. Because if you can embrace the circumstances that come your way as a chance to grow, you will experience victory no matter what you face. So what does the Lord teach you during times of adversity?

1. God Is Training You to Trust Him for All Your Needs

As we have seen throughout this study, an inward focus and self-reliant attitude can become a truly terrible form of bondage—leaving us with agonizing wounds of fear and guilt. Of course, this is where the enemy would like to keep us—limited by our own resources and unaware of all that is available through our relationship with Christ. Because of years of self-protection, we may not even realize how deeply we need the Father to redeem certain areas of our lives. We don't recognize it, that is, until we experience trials that are far beyond what we can handle.

To rid you of that internal prison, the Lord allows you to face situations where you have absolutely no choice but to rely upon Him. Slowly but surely He reveals Himself to you—demonstrating His love, character, wisdom, power, and faithfulness in meaningful ways and releasing you from the bondage to self-focus and wrongful thinking. You learn the power of His presence in your pain, the depth of His love in your loss, and His patient wisdom despite your complaints. He allows you to see that, truly, you can "stand by and see the salvation of the LORD which He will accomplish for you" (Ex. 14:13).

2. The Father Is Conforming You to the Character of Christ

Remember, the Lord's goal is to help you be like Jesus (Rom. 8:29). Instead of feeling fear, bitterness, rejection, guilt, despair, pain, and death, His desire is to produce "love, joy, peace, patience, kindness, goodness, faithfulness, gentleness, [and] self-control" (Gal. 5:22–23) in you. He wants you to overflow with the fruit of the Spirit and make you a beautiful reflection of the Savior. To do so, He must bring areas of bondage and ungodliness to the surface and purge you of them.

He wants you to overflow with the fruit of the Spirit and make you a beautiful reflection of the Savior.

This is the principle we find in Hebrews 12:10–11 which explains, "He disciplines us for our good, so that we may share His holiness. All discipline for the moment seems not to be joyful, but sorrowful; yet to those who have been trained by it, afterwards it yields the peaceful fruit of righteousness." In other words, through difficulties, He will strip you of destructive defense mechanisms, renew your passion for His purposes, refine your temperament, and purify your motives so that His very character can be seen in you.

It is not always a pleasant process—especially as He cleanses you of all the strongholds in your life—but it is most certainly the best and most worthy one you could ever hope to engage in.

3. God Uses Adversity to Prepare You for Ministry

If there is anything in this world we can all relate to, it is painful emotions and suffering. And as you seek the Father in your trials, He trains you to comfort others and proclaim the hope that He has given to you. We saw this previously as we considered 2 Corinthians 1:3–4, which says, "Blessed be the God and Father of our Lord Jesus Christ, the Father of mercies and God of all comfort, who comforts us in all our affliction so that we will be able to comfort those who are in any affliction with the comfort with which we ourselves are comforted by God." The Father makes us living vessels

Our brokenness is God's requirement for maximum usefulness.

of His consolation, wisdom, and assurance through the difficulties we face so that others can know Him and be saved.

So often we may be tempted to believe that our wounded emotions disqualify us from serving the Lord. But the truth of the matter is that our brokenness is God's requirement for maximum usefulness.

Friend, the Father has a very important plan and purpose for your life. Even in the areas where you think He cannot use you—your weaknesses, inadequacies, and even your failures—He still looks forward to exhibiting His love and grace to others through you. We know this from 2 Corinthians 12:9, where He asserts, "My . . . power is perfected in weakness." Likewise, the apostle Paul tells us, "God has chosen the weak things of the world to shame the things which are strong . . . so that no man may boast before God. But by His doing you are in Christ Jesus, who became to us wisdom from God, and righteousness and sanctification, and redemption" (1 Cor. 1:27, 29–30).

In other words, I have absolutely no doubt that He can reveal Himself even through the most emotionally painful parts of your life to reach others for His kingdom.

THE OPPORTUNITIES IN YOUR PATH

God can and will work through you, even if your situation does not appear optimal for serving Him. Of course, it is possible you may be thinking, *You just don't understand my situation, Dr. Stanley. I am still very wounded. And I have enough to do just taking care of my family, home, work, and the immense responsibilities that go with each of them. I don't have time to do anything else. I know you said God could work through me, but really, what do I have to offer? I'm not a preacher or missionary. There are many people much better able to serve the Lord than I am. He doesn't need me.*

Yes He does. You are a member of the Body of Christ, and

1 Corinthians 12:7 testifies that "to each one is given the mani-festation of the Spirit for the common good." In other words, be-cause the Holy Spirit lives in you, you are important, wanted, and absolutely needed.

God created you with a unique mix of personality, gifts, and talents to represent Him in a very special way. And because you have been bought by the blood of Christ, empowered by the Holy Spirit, and in-structed through His Word, you can be confident that you have everything you need to succeed in every good work He commissions you to carry out. That does not mean you have to preach a sermon, plant a church, or sing a solo next Sun-day—though God may call you to do one of those at some point. Rather, it means that you should be His representative and learn what He has to teach you right where you are.

> *You can be confident that you have everything you need to succeed in every good work He commissions you to carry out.*

For instance, there was a time while I was in seminary that I had a job that was far less than pleasant—in fact, it was downright terrible. I needed money to go to school, and I found employment at a food market as a cleanup boy. I had to scrub the tables and sweep up some absolutely awful messes.

I remember the first week I thought, *God, I deserve better than this.* But then I realized that the Father had called me to be a ser-vant—*His* servant—and that if I were really going to honor Him, I needed to correct my attitude. As the apostle Paul instructs in Colossians 3:23–24, "Whatever you do, do your work heartily, as for the Lord rather than for men, knowing that from the Lord you will receive the reward of the inheritance. It is the Lord Christ whom you serve."

God was cleaning me up while I was washing and tidying that store. Not only did understanding my responsibility to Him change my work, it also transformed my approach to every area of my life and how I saw others.

So what I would like you to see is that you and I are called to love and serve the Lord with all our heart, mind, soul, and strength in *every* situation—regardless if it is typical Christian service or not. The apostle Paul instructs, "Have this attitude in yourselves which was also in Christ Jesus, who . . . emptied Himself, taking the form of a bond-servant, and being made in the likeness of men . . . humbled Himself by becoming obedient to the point of death . . . on a cross" (Phil. 2:5–8).

> *You are called to love and serve the Lord with all your heart, mind, soul, and strength in every situation— regardless if it is typical Christian service or not.*

Jesus Christ came into this world as a Servant, humbly giving His life so that we would be reconciled to the Father (Mark 10:45). And God's will for every believer is that we imitate what He did for us by serving others. In the power and wisdom of the Holy Spirit, we are to perform loving acts that meet the spiritual and practical needs of those who cross our paths.

There are so many people around you in need—not just physically or financially, but emotionally and spiritually as well. Everyone you meet—Christian and non-believer alike—needs someone to encourage him or her with the genuine love of Jesus. Some pray for a friend to listen to them and help them overcome their feelings of anxiety, isolation, resentment, shame, and despair. Others are just desperate for someone to show them comfort and compassion. Then there are those souls who are seeking eternal life but have looked in all the wrong places, and it has devastated them. Galatians 6:10 instructs, "While we have opportunity, let us do good to all people, and especially to those who are of the household of the faith."

TEN TERMS FOR EFFECTIVE SERVICE

Of course, you may be wondering how you can best serve those you meet. How can you encourage them in their emotional battles and also help them follow Christ? Here are ten adverbs that describe how to minister effectively as you show His love to others:

1. *Verbally*

Tell people what you admire and appreciate about them—they need to hear it. In fact, many of the individuals you know may be under terrible pressure and emotional distress and need the encouragement. So remind them of God's love and provision, and convey your concern for their well-being.

2. *Physically*

You may come into contact with people who are anxious for someone to lend them a hand. Don't turn them away. Often what is needed is a caring hug or a simple act of service. Help them in the name of Jesus (Matt. 5:41–42).

3. *Patiently*

You know how hard it is to change your thinking when your emotions are out of control. It may take a long time to get through to some people with the truth of God's Word. But instead of giving up, continue to pray for them faithfully. You'll see it is absolutely worth it when they finally embrace His love and follow Him in obedience.

4. *Gratefully*

The truth is, you will find that some individuals are challenging to minister to—their emotional bondage is incredibly deep and their defenses are extremely difficult to overcome. Ask the Father to fill you with His love for them and help you to understand their burdens. Ask Him to fill your heart with gratefulness, then thank Him for the opportunity to encourage that hurting soul.

5. Generously

When was the last time you gave freely to another person simply because you cared? Remember, God blesses us so that we might bless others. Keep your eyes open for ways to show people His provision through sacrificial giving and express your affection to them with all generosity (1 Tim. 6:18).

6. Tenderly

Now that you know the warning signs of fear, rejection, bitterness, guilt, and despair; be sensitive to other people's emotions and pay careful attention to what they tell you. Many people have come to know Jesus as their Savior because a friend took the time to listen to them and genuinely care about their concerns.

7. Forgivingly

When you begin to feel angry or resentful toward the people the Lord has called you to encourage, remember how many times God has forgiven you. Always show compassion. You may not be able to control how others treat you, but you can choose to respond to them in a manner that honors the Father.

8. Devotedly

When you are dedicated to someone, you support and defend them when they face adversity and their emotions are especially raw. You don't abandon them when challenges or problems arise. Therefore, stand by others in their time of need. They will appreciate your loyalty, and your friendship will go a long way in helping them heal.

9. Cheerfully

Be sure to stay positive and remind others of all of the Lord's promises to them—especially when their emotions are out of control or particularly negative. Through Christ, there is always hope, regardless of the circumstances. Do your best to help others cling to that truth whenever they go through trials or experience suffering.

10. Honorably

Nothing blesses another person more than when you walk in the center of God's will and allow Him to work through you. Therefore, always make your relationship with the Father your first priority. He will guide you in how to best minister to and bless those around you.

VICTORIOUS TO THE END

Make no mistake, my friend, the proof that you are in control of your emotions rather than having your feelings dominating you is that you can employ your understanding of them for the good of others and the glory of God. This is when you know for certain that you have an "overwhelming victory" (Rom. 8:37, TLB) and are "more than [a] conqueror" (KJV).

So do you know anyone who needs your care and compassion? Is there someone who struggles with the same painful emotions you do, who would benefit from your kindness and wisdom? You simply do not know how long you have to make a difference in another person's life. So make the most of the opportunity God has given you. Share His love with others verbally, physically, patiently, gratefully, generously, tenderly, forgivingly, devotedly, cheerfully, and honorably. Be the ambassador the Father uses to care for them and show them the awesome, unconditional, sacrificial love of Christ. And observe how He changes and enriches lives through your obedience to Him.

As I said before, the Father has an important plan and purpose for your life, and I have absolutely no doubt that He can reveal Himself through you powerfully. He will not only heal you of your painful feelings, but He will use your understanding of those emotions to bless others in ways you could not possibly imagine (Eph. 3:20–21).

So love and serve Him by ministering to others. Because as Jesus said, "Whatever you did for one of the least of these brothers and sisters of mine, you did for me" (Matt. 25:40, NIV). And be assured, He will never forget the devotion you show to His name or how you demonstrate His love to others (Heb. 6:10).

Father, how grateful I am for all You have done for me and all You will continue to do through my life. Thank You for saving me and helping me find the path to victory over these feelings that are so painful and overwhelming. I confess that I have allowed them to rule me for too long. They have hurt my relationships, destroyed my joy, and prevented me from fully understanding the purposes You have planned for me. Thank You for forgiving me, Father. And thank You for teaching me how to stop these emotions from dominating my life for Your glory and the good of others.

Father, I know this is a long process and that it will take time to uproot all of the areas of hurt and bondage within me. Please continue to reveal the destructive thought patterns I have ingrained within my thinking so I can repent of them and walk in the center of Your will. I want to be Your servant and ambassador, Lord God—a vessel of Your healing to whomever crosses my path. Therefore, I bring my emotions to You and place them on Your altar as a sacrifice of obedience, trust, and praise. Please help me to love others verbally, physically, patiently, gratefully, generously, tenderly, forgivingly, devotedly, cheerfully, and honorably so they can know You as Lord and Savior and likewise be freed of the wounds they bear.

Father, I thank You for hearing my prayers and healing my damaged emotions. It is my heart's desire to walk in a manner that honors You and brings You pleasure. I am so grateful You are teaching me to take control of my emotions so I can become the joyful, fruitful believer You created me to be. Thank You for healing me, restoring my hope, and giving me purpose, Lord God. Thank You for making me more than a conqueror in this situation I once thought so insurmountable and desperate. I praise You for Your great love and for leading me—and others—into the wonderful freedom You've given.

In Jesus' holy, precious, and wonderful name I pray. Amen.

QUESTIONS FOR PERSONAL REFLECTION AND GROUP STUDY

1. How has the process of thinking through your emotions helped free you from their control? Has learning how to turn them over to God helped to change your life? How?

2. Which emotion—fear, rejection, bitterness, guilt, or discouragement—do you struggle with the most? What strategies have you learned to help heal you of that emotion?

3. What biblical truth or verse of Scripture has become most meaningful to you throughout this book? Why? Have you committed it to memory?

4. What areas of your life will require continued heal-

ing and special focus? How will you remind yourself to trust God in these areas when trials arise?

5. How will you use what you've learned to glorify God in the days and years to come? Make sure to outline steps that are both achievable and sustainable.

6. Are you now able to identify these emotions in other people? If so, are you willing to share what you've learned in order to help them find freedom as well?

7. Pray—thanking the Father for what He has taught you and committing yourself to be a vessel of His grace and truth regardless of what may come.

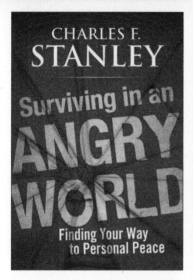
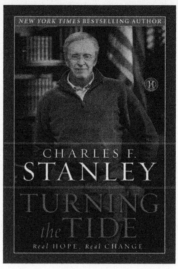
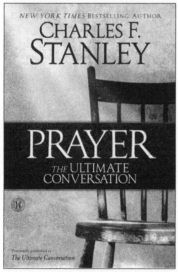

Have a "quiet time" moment.

Subscribe to the In Touch daily devotion email.
intouch.org/subscriptions